United Nations
Centre for Disarmament Affairs

DISARMAMENT

The Chemical Weapons Convention with Selective Index

United Nations, New York 1994

Editorial Note

The present publication comprises the text of the chemical weapons Convention and a selective index. The latter is intended to provide the reader with the main elements and key words and phrases of the Convention; it is based on a fuller index prepared by A. Walter Dorn and published by the United Nations Institute for Disarmament Affairs (UNIDIR) as *Index to the Chemical Weapons Convention* (Sales No. GV.E.93.0.13), Research Paper No. 18. The text of the Convention in the present volume can also be used in conjunction with the UNIDIR *Index*, as both publications utilize the pagination of the certified true copy of the Convention.

UNITED NATIONS PUBLICATION

Sales No. E.95.IX.2

ISBN 92-1-142213-2

Contents

CONVENTION ON THE PROHIBITION OF THE DEVELOPMENT, PRODUCTION,
STOCKPILING AND USE OF CHEMICAL WEAPONS AND
ON THEIR DESTRUCTION

Convention on the Prohibition of the Development, Production, Stockpiling and Use of Chemical Weapons and on Their Destruction

PREAMBLE

The States Parties to this Convention,

Determined to act with a view to achieving effective progress towards general and complete disarmament under strict and effective international control, including the prohibition and elimination of all types of weapons of mass destruction,

Desiring to contribute to the realization of the purposes and principles of the Charter of the United Nations,

Recalling that the General Assembly of the United Nations has repeatedly condemned all actions contrary to the principles and objectives of the Protocol for the Prohibition of the Use in War of Asphyxiating, Poisonous or Other Gases, and of Bacteriological Methods of Warfare, signed at Geneva on 17 June 1925 (the Geneva Protocol of 1925),

Recognizing that this Convention reaffirms principles and objectives of and obligations assumed under the Geneva Protocol of 1925, and the Convention on the Prohibition of the Development, Production and Stockpiling of Bacteriological (Biological) and Toxin Weapons and on their Destruction signed at London, Moscow and Washington on 10 April 1972,

Bearing in mind the objective contained in Article IX of the Convention on the Prohibition of the Development, Production and Stockpiling of Bacteriological (Biological) and Toxin Weapons and on their Destruction,

Determined for the sake of all mankind, to exclude completely the possibility of the use of chemical weapons, through the implementation of the provisions of this Convention, thereby complementing the obligations assumed under the Geneva Protocol of 1925,

Recognizing the prohibition, embodied in the pertinent agreements and relevant principles of international law, of the use of herbicides as a method of warfare,

Considering that achievements in the field of chemistry should be used exclusively for the benefit of mankind,

Desiring to promote free trade in chemicals as well as international cooperation and exchange of scientific and technical information in the field of chemical activities for purposes not prohibited under this Convention in order to enhance the economic and technological development of all States Parties,

Convinced that the complete and effective prohibition of the development, production, acquisition, stockpiling, retention, transfer and use of chemical weapons, and their destruction, represent a necessary step towards the achievement of these common objectives,

Have agreed as follows:

Article I

GENERAL OBLIGATIONS

1. Each State Party to this Convention undertakes never under any circumstances:

(*a*) To develop, produce, otherwise acquire, stockpile or retain chemical weapons, or transfer, directly or indirectly, chemical weapons to anyone;

(*b*) To use chemical weapons;

(*c*) To engage in any military preparations to use chemical weapons;

(*d*) To assist, encourage or induce, in any way, anyone to engage in any activity prohibited to a State Party under this Convention.

2. Each State Party undertakes to destroy chemical weapons it owns or possesses, or that are located in any place under its jurisdiction or control, in accordance with the provisions of this Convention.

3. Each State Party undertakes to destroy all chemical weapons it abandoned on the territory of another State Party, in accordance with the provisions of this Convention.

4. Each State Party undertakes to destroy any chemical weapons production facilities it owns or possesses, or that are located in any place under its jurisdiction or control, in accordance with the provisions of this Convention.

5. Each State Party undertakes not to use riot control agents as a method of warfare.

Article II

DEFINITIONS AND CRITERIA

For the purposes of this Convention:

1.   "Chemical Weapons" means the following, together or separately:

(*a*)   Toxic chemicals and their precursors, except where intended for purposes not prohibited under this Convention, as long as the types and quantities are consistent with such purposes;

(*b*)   Munitions and devices, specifically designed to cause death or other harm through the toxic properties of those toxic chemicals specified in subparagraph (*a*), which would be released as a result of the employment of such munitions and devices;

(*c*)   Any equipment specifically designed for use directly in connection with the employment of munitions and devices specified in subparagraph (*b*).

2.   "Toxic Chemical" means:

Any chemical which through its chemical action on life processes can cause death, temporary incapacitation or permanent harm to humans or animals. This includes all such chemicals, regardless of their origin or of their method of production, and regardless of whether they are produced in facilities, in munitions or elsewhere.

(For the purpose of implementing this Convention, toxic chemicals which have been identified for the application of verification measures are listed in Schedules contained in the Annex on Chemicals.)

3.   "Precursor" means:

Any chemical reactant which takes part at any stage in the production by whatever method of a toxic chemical. This includes any key component of a binary or multicomponent chemical system.

(For the purpose of implementing this Convention, precursors which have been identified for the application of verification measures are listed in Schedules contained in the Annex on Chemicals.)

4.   "Key Component of Binary or Multicomponent Chemical Systems" (hereinafter referred to as "key component") means:

The precursor which plays the most important role in determining the toxic properties of the final product and reacts rapidly with other chemicals in the binary or multicomponent system.

5.   "Old Chemical Weapons" means:

(*a*)   Chemical weapons which were produced before 1925; or

(*b*)   Chemical weapons produced in the period between 1925 and 1946 that have deteriorated to such extent that they can no longer be used as chemical weapons.

6.   "Abandoned Chemical Weapons" means:

Chemical weapons, including old chemical weapons, abandoned by a State after 1 January 1925 on the territory of another State without the consent of the latter.

7.   "Riot Control Agent" means:

Any chemical not listed in a Schedule, which can produce rapidly in humans sensory irritation or disabling physical effects which disappear within a short time following termination of exposure.

8.   "Chemical Weapons Production Facility":

(*a*)   Means any equipment, as well as any building housing such equipment, that was designed, constructed or used at any time since 1 January 1946:

   (i)   As part of the stage in the production of chemicals ("final technological stage") where the material flows would contain, when the equipment is in operation:

      (1)   Any chemical listed in Schedule 1 in the Annex on Chemicals; or

      (2)   Any other chemical that has no use, above 1 tonne per year on the territory of a State Party or in any other place under the jurisdiction or control of a State Party, for purposes not prohibited under this Convention, but can be used for chemical weapons purposes;

   or

   (ii)   For filling chemical weapons, including, *inter alia,* the filling of chemicals listed in Schedule 1 into munitions, devices or bulk storage containers; the filling of chemicals into containers that form part of assembled binary munitions and devices or into chemical submunitions that form part of assembled unitary munitions and devices, and the loading of the containers and chemical submunitions into the respective munitions and devices;

(*b*) Does not mean:

    (i)   Any facility having a production capacity for synthesis of chemicals specified in subparagraph (*a*) (i) that is less than 1 tonne;

    (ii)   Any facility in which a chemical specified in subparagraph (*a*) (i) is or was produced as an unavoidable by-product of activities for purposes not prohibited under this Convention, provided that the chemical does not exceed 3 per cent of the total product and that the facility is subject to declaration and inspection under the Annex on Implementation and Verification (hereinafter referred to as "Verification Annex"); or

    (iii)   The single small-scale facility for production of chemicals listed in Schedule 1 for purposes not prohibited under this Convention as referred to in Part VI of the Verification Annex.

9.   "Purposes Not Prohibited Under this Convention" means:

(*a*)   Industrial, agricultural, research, medical, pharmaceutical or other peaceful purposes;

(*b*)   Protective purposes, namely those purposes directly related to protection against toxic chemicals and to protection against chemical weapons;

(*c*)   Military purposes not connected with the use of chemical weapons and not dependent on the use of the toxic properties of chemicals as a method of warfare;

(*d*)   Law enforcement including domestic riot control purposes.

10.   "Production Capacity" means:

The annual quantitative potential for manufacturing a specific chemical based on the technological process actually used or, if the process is not yet operational, planned to be used at the relevant facility. It shall be deemed to be equal to the nameplate capacity or, if the nameplate capacity is not available, to the design capacity. The nameplate capacity is the product output under conditions optimized for maximum quantity for the production facility, as demonstrated by one or more test-runs. The design capacity is the corresponding theoretically calculated product output.

11.   "Organization" means the Organization for the Prohibition of Chemical Weapons established pursuant to Article VIII of this Convention.

12. For the purposes of Article VI:

(*a*)   "Production" of a chemical means its formation through chemical reaction;

(*b*)   "Processing" of a chemical means a physical process, such as formulation, extraction and purification, in which a chemical is not converted into another chemical;

(*c*)   "Consumption" of a chemical means its conversion into another chemical via a chemical reaction.

Article III

DECLARATIONS

1. Each State Party shall submit to the Organization, not later than 30 days after this Convention enters into force for it, the following declarations, in which it shall:

(*a*) With respect to chemical weapons:

    (i) Declare whether it owns or possesses any chemical weapons, or whether there are any chemical weapons located in any place under its jurisdiction or control;

    (ii) Specify the precise location, aggregate quantity and detailed inventory of chemical weapons it owns or possesses, or that are located in any place under its jurisdiction or control, in accordance with Part IV (A), paragraphs 1 to 3, of the Verification Annex, except for those chemical weapons referred to in sub-subparagraph (iii);

    (iii) Report any chemical weapons on its territory that are owned and possessed by another State and located in any place under the jurisdiction or control of another State, in accordance with Part IV (A), paragraph 4, of the Verification Annex;

    (iv) Declare whether it has transferred or received, directly or indirectly, any chemical weapons since 1 January 1946 and specify the transfer or receipt of such weapons, in accordance with Part IV (A), paragraph 5, of the Verification Annex;

    (v) Provide its general plan for destruction of chemical weapons that it owns or possesses, or that are located in any place under its jurisdiction or control, in accordance with Part IV (A), paragraph 6, of the Verification Annex;

(*b*) With respect to old chemical weapons and abandoned chemical weapons:

    (i) Declare whether it has on its territory old chemical weapons and provide all available information in accordance with Part IV (B), paragraph 3, of the Verification Annex;

(ii) Declare whether there are abandoned chemical weapons on its territory and provide all available information in accordance with Part IV (B), paragraph 8, of the Verification Annex;

(iii) Declare whether it has abandoned chemical weapons on the territory of other States and provide all available information in accordance with Part IV (B), paragraph 10, of the Verification Annex;

(c) With respect to chemical weapons production facilities:

(i) Declare whether it has or has had any chemical weapons production facility under its ownership or possession, or that is or has been located in any place under its jurisdiction or control at any time since 1 January 1946;

(ii) Specify any chemical weapons production facility it has or has had under its ownership or possession or that is or has been located in any place under its jurisdiction or control at any time since 1 January 1946, in accordance with Part V, paragraph 1, of the Verification Annex, except for those facilities referred to in sub-subparagraph (iii);

(iii) Report any chemical weapons production facility on its territory that another State has or has had under its ownership and possession and that is or has been located in any place under the jurisdiction or control of another State at any time since 1 January 1946, in accordance with Part V, paragraph 2, of the Verification Annex;

(iv) Declare whether it has transferred or received, directly or indirectly, any equipment for the production of chemical weapons since 1 January 1946 and specify the transfer or receipt of such equipment, in accordance with Part V, paragraphs 3 to 5, of the Verification Annex;

(v) Provide its general plan for destruction of any chemical weapons production facility it owns or possesses, or that is located in any place under its jurisdiction or control, in accordance with Part V, paragraph 6, of the Verification Annex;

(vi) Specify actions to be taken for closure of any chemical weapons production facility it owns or possesses, or that is located in any place under its jurisdiction or control, in accordance with Part V, paragraph 1 (i), of the Verification Annex;

(vii) Provide its general plan for any temporary conversion of any chemical weapons production facility it owns or possesses, or that is located in any place under its jurisdiction or control, into a chemical weapons destruction facility, in accordance with Part V, paragraph 7, of the Verification Annex;

(*d*)   With respect to other facilities:

Specify the precise location, nature and general scope of activities of any facility or establishment under its ownership or possession, or located in any place under its jurisdiction or control, and that has been designed, constructed or used since 1 January 1946 primarily for development of chemical weapons. Such declaration shall include, *inter alia,* laboratories and test and evaluation sites;

(*e*)   With respect to riot control agents: Specify the chemical name, structural formula and Chemical Abstracts Service (CAS) registry number, if assigned, of each chemical it holds for riot control purposes. This declaration shall be updated not later than 30 days after any change becomes effective.

2.   The provisions of this Article and the relevant provisions of Part IV of the Verification Annex shall not, at the discretion of a State Party, apply to chemical weapons buried on its territory before 1 January 1977 and which remain buried, or which had been dumped at sea before 1 January 1985.

Article IV

CHEMICAL WEAPONS

1.   The provisions of this Article and the detailed procedures for its implementation shall apply to all chemical weapons owned or possessed by a State Party, or that are located in any place under its jurisdiction or control, except old chemical weapons and abandoned chemical weapons to which Part IV (B) of the Verification Annex applies.

2.   Detailed procedures for the implementation of this Article are set forth in the Verification Annex.

3.   All locations at which chemical weapons specified in paragraph 1 are stored or destroyed shall be subject to systematic verification through on-site inspection and monitoring with on-site instruments, in accordance with Part IV (A) of the Verification Annex.

4.   Each State Party shall, immediately after the declaration under Article III, paragraph 1 (*a*), has been submitted, provide access to chemical weapons specified in paragraph 1 for the purpose of systematic verification of the declaration through on-site inspection. Thereafter, each State Party shall not remove any of these chemical weapons, except to a chemical weapons destruction facility. It shall provide access to such chemical weapons, for the purpose of systematic on-site verification.

5.   Each State Party shall provide access to any chemical weapons destruction facilities and their storage areas, that it owns or possesses, or that are located in any place under its jurisdiction or control, for the purpose of systematic verification through on-site inspection and monitoring with on-site instruments.

6.   Each State Party shall destroy all chemical weapons specified in paragraph 1 pursuant to the Verification Annex and in accordance with the agreed rate and sequence of destruction (hereinafter referred to as "order of destruction"). Such destruction shall begin not later than two years after this Convention enters into force for it and shall finish not later than 10 years after entry into force of this Convention. A State Party is not precluded from destroying such chemical weapons at a faster rate.

7.   Each State Party shall:

(*a*)   Submit detailed plans for the destruction of chemical weapons specified in paragraph 1 not later than 60 days before each annual destruction period begins, in accordance with Part IV (A), paragraph 29, of the Verification Annex; the detailed plans shall encompass all stocks to be destroyed during the next annual destruction period;

(*b*) Submit declarations annually regarding the implementation of its plans for destruction of chemical weapons specified in paragraph 1, not later than 60 days after the end of each annual destruction period; and

(*c*) Certify, not later than 30 days after the destruction process has been completed, that all chemical weapons specified in paragraph 1 have been destroyed.

8. If a State ratifies or accedes to this Convention after the 10-year period for destruction set forth in paragraph 6, it shall destroy chemical weapons specified in paragraph 1 as soon as possible. The order of destruction and procedures for stringent verification for such a State Party shall be determined by the Executive Council.

9. Any chemical weapons discovered by a State Party after the initial declaration of chemical weapons shall be reported, secured and destroyed in accordance with Part IV (A) of the Verification Annex.

10. Each State Party, during transportation, sampling, storage and destruction of chemical weapons, shall assign the highest priority to ensuring the safety of people and to protecting the environment. Each State Party shall transport, sample, store and destroy chemical weapons in accordance with its national standards for safety and emissions.

11. Any State Party which has on its territory chemical weapons that are owned or possessed by another State, or that are located in any place under the jurisdiction or control of another State, shall make the fullest efforts to ensure that these chemical weapons are removed from its territory not later than one year after this Convention enters into force for it. If they are not removed within one year, the State Party may request the Organization and other States Parties to provide assistance in the destruction of these chemical weapons.

12. Each State Party undertakes to cooperate with other States Parties that request information or assistance on a bilateral basis or through the Technical Secretariat regarding methods and technologies for the safe and efficient destruction of chemical weapons.

13. In carrying out verification activities pursuant to this Article and Part IV (A) of the Verification Annex, the Organization shall consider measures to avoid unnecessary duplication of bilateral or multilateral agreements on verification of chemical weapons storage and their destruction among States Parties.

To this end, the Executive Council shall decide to limit verification to measures complementary to those undertaken pursuant to such a bilateral or multilateral agreement, if it considers that:

(*a*)   Verification provisions of such an agreement are consistent with the verification provisions of this Article and Part IV (A) of the Verification Annex;

(*b*)   Implementation of such an agreement provides for sufficient assurance of compliance with the relevant provisions of this Convention; and

(*c*)   Parties to the bilateral or multilateral agreement keep the Organization fully informed about their verification activities.

14.   If the Executive Council takes a decision pursuant to paragraph 13, the Organization shall have the right to monitor the implementation of the bilateral or multilateral agreement.

15.   Nothing in paragraphs 13 and 14 shall affect the obligation of a State Party to provide declarations pursuant to Article III, this Article and Part IV (A) of the Verification Annex.

16.   Each State Party shall meet the costs of destruction of chemical weapons it is obliged to destroy. It shall also meet the costs of verification of storage and destruction of these chemical weapons unless the Executive Council decides otherwise. If the Executive Council decides to limit verification measures of the Organization pursuant to paragraph 13, the costs of complementary verification and monitoring by the Organization shall be paid in accordance with the United Nations scale of assessment, as specified in Article VIII, paragraph 7.

17.   The provisions of this Article and the relevant provisions of Part IV of the Verification Annex shall not, at the discretion of a State Party, apply to chemical weapons buried on its territory before 1 January 1977 and which remain buried, or which had been dumped at sea before 1 January 1985.

Article V

CHEMICAL WEAPONS PRODUCTION FACILITIES

1.   The provisions of this Article and the detailed procedures for its implementation shall apply to any and all chemical weapons production facilities owned or possessed by a State Party, or that are located in any place under its jurisdiction or control.

2.   Detailed procedures for the implementation of this Article are set forth in the Verification Annex.

3.   All chemical weapons production facilities specified in paragraph 1 shall be subject to systematic verification through on-site inspection and monitoring with on-site instruments in accordance with Part V of the Verification Annex.

4.   Each State Party shall cease immediately all activity at chemical weapons production facilities specified in paragraph 1, except activity required for closure.

5.   No State Party shall construct any new chemical weapons production facilities or modify any existing facilities for the purpose of chemical weapons production or for any other activity prohibited under this Convention.

6.   Each State Party shall, immediately after the declaration under Article III, paragraph 1 *(c)*, has been submitted, provide access to chemical weapons production facilities specified in paragraph 1, for the purpose of systematic verification of the declaration through on-site inspection.

7.   Each State Party shall:

(a)   Close, not later than 90 days after this Convention enters into force for it, all chemical weapons production facilities specified in paragraph 1, in accordance with Part V of the Verification Annex, and give notice thereof; and

(b)   Provide access to chemical weapons production facilities specified in paragraph 1, subsequent to closure, for the purpose of systematic verification through on-site inspection and monitoring with on-site instruments in order to ensure that the facility remains closed and is subsequently destroyed.

8.   Each State Party shall destroy all chemical weapons production facilities specified in paragraph 1 and related facilities and equipment, pursuant to the Verification Annex and in accordance with an agreed rate and sequence of destruction (hereinafter referred to as "order of destruction"). Such destruction shall begin not later than one year after this Convention enters into force for it, and shall finish not later than 10 years after entry into force of this Convention. A State Party is not precluded from destroying such facilities at a faster rate.

9. Each State Party shall:

(a) Submit detailed plans for destruction of chemical weapons production facilities specified in paragraph 1, not later than 180 days before the destruction of each facility begins;

(b) Submit declarations annually regarding the implementation of its plans for the destruction of all chemical weapons production facilities specified in paragraph 1, not later than 90 days after the end of each annual destruction period; and

(c) Certify, not later than 30 days after the destruction process has been completed, that all chemical weapons production facilities specified in paragraph 1 have been destroyed.

10. If a State ratifies or accedes to this Convention after the 10-year period for destruction set forth in paragraph 8, it shall destroy chemical weapons production facilities specified in paragraph 1 as soon as possible. The order of destruction and procedures for stringent verification for such a State Party shall be determined by the Executive Council.

11. Each State Party, during the destruction of chemical weapons production facilities, shall assign the highest priority to ensuring the safety of people and to protecting the environment. Each State Party shall destroy chemical weapons production facilities in accordance with its national standards for safety and emissions.

12. Chemical weapons production facilities specified in paragraph 1 may be temporarily converted for destruction of chemical weapons in accordance with Part V, paragraphs 18 to 25, of the Verification Annex. Such a converted facility must be destroyed as soon as it is no longer in use for destruction of chemical weapons but, in any case, not later than 10 years after entry into force of this Convention.

13. A State Party may request, in exceptional cases of compelling need, permission to use a chemical weapons production facility specified in paragraph 1 for purposes not prohibited under this Convention. Upon the recommendation of the Executive Council, the Conference of the States Parties shall decide whether or not to approve the request and shall establish the conditions upon which approval is contingent in accordance with Part V, Section D, of the Verification Annex.

14. The chemical weapons production facility shall be converted in such a manner that the converted facility is not more capable of being reconverted into a chemical weapons production facility than any other facility used for industrial, agricultural, research, medical, pharmaceutical or other peaceful purposes not involving chemicals listed in Schedule 1.

15. All converted facilities shall be subject to systematic verification through on-site inspection and monitoring with on-site instruments in accordance with Part V, Section D, of the Verification Annex.

16. In carrying out verification activities pursuant to this Article and Part V of the Verification Annex, the Organization shall consider measures to avoid unnecessary duplication of bilateral or multilateral agreements on verification of chemical weapons production facilities and their destruction among States Parties.

To this end, the Executive Council shall decide to limit the verification to measures complementary to those undertaken pursuant to such a bilateral or multilateral agreement, if it considers that:

(*a*) Verification provisions of such an agreement are consistent with the verification provisions of this Article and Part V of the Verification Annex;

(*b*) Implementation of the agreement provides for sufficient assurance of compliance with the relevant provisions of this Convention; and

(*c*) Parties to the bilateral or multilateral agreement keep the Organization fully informed about their verification activities.

17. If the Executive Council takes a decision pursuant to paragraph 16, the Organization shall have the right to monitor the implementation of the bilateral or multilateral agreement.

18. Nothing in paragraphs 16 and 17 shall affect the obligation of a State Party to make declarations pursuant to Article III, this Article and Part V of the Verification Annex.

19. Each State Party shall meet the costs of destruction of chemical weapons production facilities it is obliged to destroy. It shall also meet the costs of verification under this Article unless the Executive Council decides otherwise. If the Executive Council decides to limit verification measures of the Organization pursuant to paragraph 16, the costs of complementary verification and monitoring by the Organization shall be paid in accordance with the United Nations scale of assessment, as specified in Article VIII, paragraph 7.

Article VI

ACTIVITIES NOT PROHIBITED UNDER THIS CONVENTION

1.   Each State Party has the right, subject to the provisions of this Convention, to develop, produce, otherwise acquire, retain, transfer and use toxic chemicals and their precursors for purposes not prohibited under this Convention.

2.   Each State Party shall adopt the necessary measures to ensure that toxic chemicals and their precursors are only developed, produced, otherwise acquired, retained, transferred, or used within its territory or in any other place under its jurisdiction or control for purposes not prohibited under this Convention. To this end, and in order to verify that activities are in accordance with obligations under this Convention, each State Party shall subject toxic chemicals and their precursors listed in Schedules 1, 2 and 3 of the Annex on Chemicals, facilities related to such chemicals, and other facilities as specified in the Verification Annex, that are located on its territory or in any other place under its jurisdiction or control, to verification measures as provided in the Verification Annex.

3.   Each State Party shall subject chemicals listed in Schedule 1 (hereinafter referred to as "Schedule 1 chemicals") to the prohibitions on production, acquisition, retention, transfer and use as specified in Part VI of the Verification Annex. It shall subject Schedule 1 chemicals and facilities specified in Part VI of the Verification Annex to systematic verification through on-site inspection and monitoring with on-site instruments in accordance with that Part of the Verification Annex.

4.   Each State Party shall subject chemicals listed in Schedule 2 (hereinafter referred to as "Schedule 2 chemicals") and facilities specified in Part VII of the Verification Annex to data monitoring and on-site verification in accordance with that Part of the Verification Annex.

5.   Each State Party shall subject chemicals listed in Schedule 3 (hereinafter referred to as "Schedule 3 chemicals") and facilities specified in Part VIII of the Verification Annex to data monitoring and on-site verification in accordance with that Part of the Verification Annex.

6.   Each State Party shall subject facilities specified in Part IX of the Verification Annex to data monitoring and eventual on-site verification in accordance with that Part of the Verification Annex unless decided otherwise by the Conference of the States Parties pursuant to Part IX, paragraph 22, of the Verification Annex.

7. Not later than 30 days after this Convention enters into force for it, each State Party shall make an initial declaration on relevant chemicals and facilities in accordance with the Verification Annex.

8. Each State Party shall make annual declarations regarding the relevant chemicals and facilities in accordance with the Verification Annex.

9. For the purpose of on-site verification, each State Party shall grant to the inspectors access to facilities as required in the Verification Annex.

10. In conducting verification activities, the Technical Secretariat shall avoid undue intrusion into the State Party's chemical activities for purposes not prohibited under this Convention and, in particular, abide by the provisions set forth in the Annex on the Protection of Confidential Information (hereinafter referred to as "Confidentiality Annex").

11. The provisions of this Article shall be implemented in a manner which avoids hampering the economic or technological development of States Parties, and international cooperation in the field of chemical activities for purposes not prohibited under this Convention including the international exchange of scientific and technical information and chemicals and equipment for the production, processing or use of chemicals for purposes not prohibited under this Convention.

Article VII

NATIONAL IMPLEMENTATION MEASURES

General undertakings

1.   Each State Party shall, in accordance with its constitutional processes, adopt the necessary measures to implement its obligations under this Convention. In particular, it shall:

(*a*)   Prohibit natural and legal persons anywhere on its territory or in any other place under its jurisdiction as recognized by international law from undertaking any activity prohibited to a State Party under this Convention, including enacting penal legislation with respect to such activity;

(*b*)   Not permit in any place under its control any activity prohibited to a State Party under this Convention; and

(*c*)   Extend its penal legislation enacted under subparagraph (*a*) to any activity prohibited to a State Party under this Convention undertaken anywhere by natural persons, possessing its nationality, in conformity with international law.

2.   Each State Party shall cooperate with other States Parties and afford the appropriate form of legal assistance to facilitate the implementation of the obligations under paragraph 1.

3.   Each State Party, during the implementation of its obligations under this Convention, shall assign the highest priority to ensuring the safety of people and to protecting the environment, and shall cooperate as appropriate with other States Parties in this regard.

Relations between the State Party and the Organization

4.   In order to fulfil its obligations under this Convention, each State Party shall designate or establish a National Authority to serve as the national focal point for effective liaison with the Organization and other States Parties. Each State Party shall notify the Organization of its National Authority at the time that this Convention enters into force for it.

5.   Each State Party shall inform the Organization of the legislative and administrative measures taken to implement this Convention.

6.   Each State Party shall treat as confidential and afford special handling to information and data that it receives in confidence from the Organization in connection with the implementation of this Convention. It shall treat such

information and data exclusively in connection with its rights and obligations under this Convention and in accordance with the provisions set forth in the Confidentiality Annex.

7.   Each State Party undertakes to cooperate with the Organization in the exercise of all its functions and in particular to provide assistance to the Technical Secretariat.

Article VIII

THE ORGANIZATION

A. GENERAL PROVISIONS

1. The States Parties to this Convention hereby establish the Organization for the Prohibition of Chemical Weapons to achieve the object and purpose of this Convention, to ensure the implementation of its provisions, including those for international verification of compliance with it, and to provide a forum for consultation and cooperation among States Parties.

2. All States Parties to this Convention shall be members of the Organization. A State Party shall not be deprived of its membership in the Organization.

3. The seat of the Headquarters of the Organization shall be The Hague, Kingdom of the Netherlands.

4. There are hereby established as the organs of the Organization: the Conference of the States Parties, the Executive Council, and the Technical Secretariat.

5. The Organization shall conduct its verification activities provided for under this Convention in the least intrusive manner possible consistent with the timely and efficient accomplishment of their objectives. It shall request only the information and data necessary to fulfil its responsibilities under this Convention. It shall take every precaution to protect the confidentiality of information on civil and military activities and facilities coming to its knowledge in the implementation of this Convention and, in particular, shall abide by the provisions set forth in the Confidentiality Annex.

6. In undertaking its verification activities the Organization shall consider measures to make use of advances in science and technology.

7. The costs of the Organization's activities shall be paid by States Parties in accordance with the United Nations scale of assessment adjusted to take into account differences in membership between the United Nations and this Organization, and subject to the provisions of Articles IV and V. Financial contributions of States Parties to the Preparatory Commission shall be deducted in an appropriate way from their contributions to the regular budget. The budget of the Organization shall comprise two separate chapters, one relating to administrative and other costs, and one relating to verification costs.

8. A member of the Organization which is in arrears in the payment of its financial contribution to the Organization shall have no vote in the Organization if the amount of its arrears equals or exceeds the amount of the contribution due

from it for the preceding two full years. The Conference of the States Parties may, nevertheless, permit such a member to vote if it is satisfied that the failure to pay is due to conditions beyond the control of the member.

B. THE CONFERENCE OF THE STATES PARTIES

Composition, procedures and decision-making

9. The Conference of the States Parties (hereinafter referred to as "the Conference") shall be composed of all members of this Organization. Each member shall have one representative in the Conference, who may be accompanied by alternates and advisers.

10. The first session of the Conference shall be convened by the depositary not later than 30 days after the entry into force of this Convention.

11. The Conference shall meet in regular sessions which shall be held annually unless it decides otherwise.

12. Special sessions of the Conference shall be convened:

(*a*)   When decided by the Conference;

(*b*)   When requested by the Executive Council;

(*c*)   When requested by any member and supported by one third of the members; or

(*d*) In accordance with paragraph 22 to undertake reviews of the operation of this Convention.

Except in the case of subparagraph (*d*), the special session shall be convened not later than 30 days after receipt of the request by the Director-General of the Technical Secretariat, unless specified otherwise in the request.

13. The Conference shall also be convened in the form of an Amendment Conference in accordance with Article XV, paragraph 2.

14. Sessions of the Conference shall take place at the seat of the Organization unless the Conference decides otherwise.

15. The Conference shall adopt its rules of procedure. At the beginning of each regular session, it shall elect its Chairman and such other officers as may be required. They shall hold office until a new Chairman and other officers are elected at the next regular session.

16.   A majority of the members of the Organization shall constitute a quorum for the Conference.

17.   Each member of the Organization shall have one vote in the Conference.

18.   The Conference shall take decisions on questions of procedure by a simple majority of the members present and voting. Decisions on matters of substance should be taken as far as possible by consensus. If consensus is not attainable when an issue comes up for decision, the Chairman shall defer any vote for 24 hours and during this period of deferment shall make every effort to facilitate achievement of consensus, and shall report to the Conference before the end of this period. If consensus is not possible at the end of 24 hours, the Conference shall take the decision by a two-thirds majority of members present and voting unless specified otherwise in this Convention. When the issue arises as to whether the question is one of substance or not, that question shall be treated as a matter of substance unless otherwise decided by the Conference by the majority required for decisions on matters of substance.

Powers and functions

19.   The Conference shall be the principal organ of the Organization. It shall consider any questions, matters or issues within the scope of this Convention, including those relating to the powers and functions of the Executive Council and the Technical Secretariat. It may make recommendations and take decisions on any questions, matters or issues related to this Convention raised by a State Party or brought to its attention by the Executive Council.

20.   The Conference shall oversee the implementation of this Convention, and act in order to promote its object and purpose. The Conference shall review compliance with this Convention. It shall also oversee the activities of the Executive Council and the Technical Secretariat and may issue guidelines in accordance with this Convention to either of them in the exercise of their functions.

21.   The Conference shall:

(*a*)   Consider and adopt at its regular sessions the report, programme and budget of the Organization, submitted by the Executive Council, as well as consider other reports;

(*b*)   Decide on the scale of financial contributions to be paid by States Parties in accordance with paragraph 7;

(*c*)   Elect the members of the Executive Council;

(*d*)   Appoint the Director-General of the Technical Secretariat (hereinafter referred to as "the Director-General");

(*e*)   Approve the rules of procedure of the Executive Council submitted by the latter;

(*f*)   Establish such subsidiary organs as it finds necessary for the exercise of its functions in accordance with this Convention;

(*g*)   Foster international cooperation for peaceful purposes in the field of chemical activities;

(*h*)   Review scientific and technological developments that could affect the operation of this Convention and, in this context, direct the Director-General to establish a Scientific Advisory Board to enable him, in the performance of his functions, render specialized advice in areas of science and technology relevant to this Convention, to the Conference, the Executive Council or States Parties. The Scientific Advisory Board shall be composed of independent experts appointed in accordance with terms of reference adopted by the Conference;

(*i*)   Consider and approve at its first session any draft agreements, provisions and guidelines developed by the Preparatory Commission;

(*j*)   Establish at its first session the voluntary fund for assistance in accordance with Article X;

(*k*)   Take the necessary measures to ensure compliance with this Convention and to redress and remedy any situation which contravenes the provisions of this Convention, in accordance with Article XII.

22.   The Conference shall not later than one year after the expiry of the fifth and the tenth year after the entry into force of this Convention, and at such other times within that time period as may be decided upon, convene in special sessions to undertake reviews of the operation of this Convention. Such reviews shall take into account any relevant scientific and technological developments. At intervals of five years thereafter, unless otherwise decided upon, further sessions of the Conference shall be convened with the same objective.

C.   The Executive Council

Composition, procedure and decision-making

23.   The Executive Council shall consist of 41 members. Each State Party shall have the right, in accordance with the principle of rotation, to serve on the Executive Council. The members of the Executive Council shall be elected

by the Conference for a term of two years. In order to ensure the effective functioning of this Convention, due regard being specially paid to equitable geographical distribution, to the importance of chemical industry, as well as to political and security interests, the Executive Council shall be composed as follows:

(a)   Nine States Parties from Africa to be designated by States Parties located in this region. As a basis for this designation it is understood that, out of these nine States Parties, three members shall, as a rule, be the States Parties with the most significant national chemical industry in the region as determined by internationally reported and published data; in addition, the regional group shall agree also to take into account other regional factors in designating these three members;

(b)   Nine States Parties from Asia to be designated by States Parties located in this region. As a basis for this designation it is understood that, out of these nine States Parties, four members shall, as a rule, be the States Parties with the most significant national chemical industry in the region as determined by internationally reported and published data; in addition, the regional group shall agree also to take into account other regional factors in designating these four members;

(c)   Five States Parties from Eastern Europe to be designated by States Parties located in this region. As a basis for this designation it is understood that, out of these five States Parties, one member shall, as a rule, be the State Party with the most significant national chemical industry in the region as determined by internationally reported and published data; in addition, the regional group shall agree also to take into account other regional factors in designating this one member;

(d)   Seven States Parties from Latin America and the Caribbean to be designated by States Parties located in this region. As a basis for this designation it is understood that, out of these seven States Parties, three members shall, as a rule, be the States Parties with the most significant national chemical industry in the region as determined by internationally reported and published data; in addition, the regional group shall agree also to take into account other regional factors in designating these three members;

(e)   Ten States Parties from among Western European and other States to be designated by States Parties located in this region. As a basis for this designation it is understood that, out of these 10 States Parties, 5 members shall, as a rule, be the States Parties with the most significant national chemical industry in the region as determined by internationally reported and published data; in addition, the regional group shall agree also to take into account other regional factors in designating these five members;

(*f*)   One further State Party to be designated consecutively by States Parties located in the regions of Asia and Latin America and the Caribbean. As a basis for this designation it is understood that this State Party shall be a rotating member from these regions.

24. For the first election of the Executive Council 20 members shall be elected for a term of one year, due regard being paid to the established numerical proportions as described in paragraph 23.

25. After the full implementation of Articles IV and V the Conference may, upon the request of a majority of the members of the Executive Council, review the composition of the Executive Council taking into account developments related to the principles specified in paragraph 23 that are governing its composition.

26. The Executive Council shall elaborate its rules of procedure and submit them to the Conference for approval.

27. The Executive Council shall elect its Chairman from among its members.

28. The Executive Council shall meet for regular sessions. Between regular sessions it shall meet as often as may be required for the fulfilment of its powers and functions.

29. Each member of the Executive Council shall have one vote. Unless otherwise specified in this Convention, the Executive Council shall take decisions on matters of substance by a two-thirds majority of all its members. The Executive Council shall take decisions on questions of procedure by a simple majority of all its members. When the issue arises as to whether the question is one of substance or not, that question shall be treated as a matter of substance unless otherwise decided by the Executive Council by the majority required for decisions on matters of substance.

Powers and functions

30. The Executive Council shall be the executive organ of the Organization. It shall be responsible to the Conference. The Executive Council shall carry out the powers and functions entrusted to it under this Convention, as well as those functions delegated to it by the Conference. In so doing, it shall act in conformity with the recommendations, decisions and guidelines of the Conference and assure their proper and continuous implementation.

31. The Executive Council shall promote the effective implementation of, and compliance with, this Convention. It shall supervise the activities of the Technical Secretariat, cooperate with the National Authority of each State Party and facilitate consultations and cooperation among States Parties at their request.

32. The Executive Council shall:

(*a*) Consider and submit to the Conference the draft programme and budget of the Organization;

(*b*) Consider and submit to the Conference the draft report of the Organization on the implementation of this Convention, the report on the performance of its own activities and such special reports as it deems necessary or which the Conference may request;

(*c*) Make arrangements for the sessions of the Conference including the preparation of the draft agenda.

33. The Executive Council may request the convening of a special session of the Conference.

34. The Executive Council shall:

(*a*) Conclude agreements or arrangements with States and international organizations on behalf of the Organization, subject to prior approval by the Conference;

(*b*) Conclude agreements with States Parties on behalf of the Organization in connection with Article X and supervise the voluntary fund referred to in Article X;

(*c*) Approve agreements or arrangements relating to the implementation of verification activities, negotiated by the Technical Secretariat with States Parties.

35. The Executive Council shall consider any issue or matter within its competence affecting this Convention and its implementation, including concerns regarding compliance, and cases of non-compliance, and, as appropriate, inform States Parties and bring the issue or matter to the attention of the Conference.

36. In its consideration of doubts or concerns regarding compliance and cases of non-compliance, including, *inter alia,* abuse of the rights provided for under this Convention, the Executive Council shall consult with the States Parties involved and, as appropriate, request the State Party to take measures to redress the situation within a specified time. To the extent that the Executive Council considers further action to be necessary, it shall take, *inter alia,* one or more of the following measures:

(*a*) Inform all States Parties of the issue or matter;

(*b*) Bring the issue or matter to the attention of the Conference;

(*c*)   Make recommendations to the Conference regarding measures to redress the situation and to ensure compliance.

The Executive Council shall, in cases of particular gravity and urgency, bring the issue or matter, including relevant information and conclusions, directly to the attention of the United Nations General Assembly and the United Nations Security Council. It shall at the same time inform all States Parties of this step.

D.   THE TECHNICAL SECRETARIAT

37.   The Technical Secretariat shall assist the Conference and the Executive Council in the performance of their functions. The Technical Secretariat shall carry out the verification measures provided for in this Convention. It shall carry out the other functions entrusted to it under this Convention as well as those functions delegated to it by the Conference and the Executive Council.

38.   The Technical Secretariat shall:

(*a*)   Prepare and submit to the Executive Council the draft programme and budget of the Organization;

(*b*)   Prepare and submit to the Executive Council the draft report of the Organization on the implementation of this Convention and such other reports as the Conference or the Executive Council may request;

(*c*)   Provide administrative and technical support to the Conference, the Executive Council and subsidiary organs;

(*d*)   Address and receive communications on behalf of the Organization to and from States Parties on matters pertaining to the implementation of this Convention;

(*e*)   Provide technical assistance and technical evaluation to States Parties in the implementation of the provisions of this Convention, including evaluation of scheduled and unscheduled chemicals.

39.   The Technical Secretariat shall:

(*a*)   Negotiate agreements or arrangements relating to the implementation of verification activities with States Parties, subject to approval by the Executive Council;

(*b*)   Not later than 180 days after entry into force of this Convention, coordinate the establishment and maintenance of permanent stockpiles of emergency and humanitarian assistance by States Parties in accordance with

Article X, paragraphs 7 (*b*) and (*c*). The Technical Secretariat may inspect the items maintained for serviceability. Lists of items to be stockpiled shall be considered and approved by the Conference pursuant to paragraph 21 (*i*) above;

(*c*)   Administer the voluntary fund referred to in Article X, compile declarations made by the States Parties and register, when requested, bilateral agreements concluded between States Parties or between a State Party and the Organization for the purposes of Article X.

40.   The Technical Secretariat shall inform the Executive Council of any problem that has arisen with regard to the discharge of its functions, including doubts, ambiguities or uncertainties about compliance with this Convention that have come to its notice in the performance of its verification activities and that it has been unable to resolve or clarify through its consultations with the State Party concerned.

41.   The Technical Secretariat shall comprise a Director-General, who shall be its head and chief administrative officer, inspectors and such scientific, technical and other personnel as may be required.

42.   The Inspectorate shall be a unit of the Technical Secretariat and shall act under the supervision of the Director-General.

43.   The Director-General shall be appointed by the Conference upon the recommendation of the Executive Council for a term of four years, renewable for one further term, but not thereafter.

44.   The Director-General shall be responsible to the Conference and the Executive Council for the appointment of the staff and the organization and functioning of the Technical Secretariat. The paramount consideration in the employment of the staff and in the determination of the conditions of service shall be the necessity of securing the highest standards of efficiency, competence and integrity. Only citizens of States Parties shall serve as the Director-General, as inspectors or as other members of the professional and clerical staff. Due regard shall be paid to the importance of recruiting the staff on as wide a geographical basis as possible. Recruitment shall be guided by the principle that the staff shall be kept to a minimum necessary for the proper discharge of the responsibilities of the Technical Secretariat.

45.   The Director-General shall be responsible for the organization and functioning of the Scientific Advisory Board referred to in paragraph 21 (*h*). The Director-General shall, in consultation with States Parties, appoint members of the Scientific Advisory Board, who shall serve in their individual capacity. The members of the Board shall be appointed on the basis of their expertise in the particular

scientific fields relevant to the implementation of this Convention. The Director-General may also, as appropriate, in consultation with members of the Board, establish temporary working groups of scientific experts to provide recommendations on specific issues. In regard to the above, States Parties may submit lists of experts to the Director-General.

46. In the performance of their duties, the Director-General, the inspectors and the other members of the staff shall not seek or receive instructions from any Government or from any other source external to the Organization. They shall refrain from any action that might reflect on their positions as international officers responsible only to the Conference and the Executive Council.

47. Each State Party shall respect the exclusively international character of the responsibilities of the Director-General, the inspectors and the other members of the staff and not seek to influence them in the discharge of their responsibilities.

E. PRIVILEGES AND IMMUNITIES

48. The Organization shall enjoy on the territory and in any other place under the jurisdiction or control of a State Party such legal capacity and such privileges and immunities as are necessary for the exercise of its functions.

49. Delegates of States Parties, together with their alternates and advisers, representatives appointed to the Executive Council together with their alternates and advisers, the Director-General and the staff of the Organization shall enjoy such privileges and immunities as are necessary in the independent exercise of their functions in connection with the Organization.

50. The legal capacity, privileges, and immunities referred to in this Article shall be defined in agreements between the Organization and the States Parties as well as in an agreement between the Organization and the State in which the headquarters of the Organization is seated. These agreements shall be considered and approved by the Conference pursuant to paragraph 21 (*i*).

51. Notwithstanding paragraphs 48 and 49, the privileges and immunities enjoyed by the Director-General and the staff of the Technical Secretariat during the conduct of verification activities shall be those set forth in Part II, Section B, of the Verification Annex.

Article IX

CONSULTATIONS, COOPERATION AND FACT-FINDING

1.   States Parties shall consult and cooperate, directly among themselves, or through the Organization or other appropriate international procedures, including procedures within the framework of the United Nations and in accordance with its Charter, on any matter which may be raised relating to the object and purpose, or the implementation of the provisions, of this Convention.

2.   Without prejudice to the right of any State Party to request a challenge inspection, States Parties should, whenever possible, first make every effort to clarify and resolve, through exchange of information and consultations among themselves, any matter which may cause doubt about compliance with this Convention, or which gives rise to concerns about a related matter which may be considered ambiguous. A State Party which receives a request from another State Party for clarification of any matter which the requesting State Party believes causes such a doubt or concern shall provide the requesting State Party as soon as possible, but in any case not later than 10 days after the request, with information sufficient to answer the doubt or concern raised along with an explanation of how the information provided resolves the matter. Nothing in this Convention shall affect the right of any two or more States Parties to arrange by mutual consent for inspections or any other procedures among themselves to clarify and resolve any matter which may cause doubt about compliance or gives rise to a concern about a related matter which may be considered ambiguous. Such arrangements shall not affect the rights and obligations of any State Party under other provisions of this Convention.

Procedure for requesting clarification

3.   A State Party shall have the right to request the Executive Council to assist in clarifying any situation which may be considered ambiguous or which gives rise to a concern about the possible non-compliance of another State Party with this Convention. The Executive Council shall provide appropriate information in its possession relevant to such a concern.

4.   A State Party shall have the right to request the Executive Council to obtain clarification from another State Party on any situation which may be considered ambiguous or which gives rise to a concern about its possible non-compliance with this Convention. In such a case, the following shall apply:

(*a*)   The Executive Council shall forward the request for clarification to the State Party concerned through the Director-General not later than 24 hours after its receipt;

(*b*)   The requested State Party shall provide the clarification to the Executive Council as soon as possible, but in any case not later than 10 days after the receipt of the request;

(*c*)   The Executive Council shall take note of the clarification and forward it to the requesting State Party not later than 24 hours after its receipt;

(*d*) If the requesting State Party deems the clarification to be inadequate, it shall have the right to request the Executive Council to obtain from the requested State Party further clarification;

(*e*)   For the purpose of obtaining further clarification requested under subparagraph (*d*), the Executive Council may call on the Director-General to establish a group of experts from the Technical Secretariat, or if appropriate staff are not available in the Technical Secretariat, from elsewhere, to examine all available information and data relevant to the situation causing the concern. The group of experts shall submit a factual report to the Executive Council on its findings;

(*f*)   If the requesting State Party considers the clarification obtained under subparagraphs (*d*) and (*e*) to be unsatisfactory, it shall have the right to request a special session of the Executive Council in which States Parties involved that are not members of the Executive Council shall be entitled to take part. In such a special session, the Executive Council shall consider the matter and may recommend any measure it deems appropriate to resolve the situation.

5.   A State Party shall also have the right to request the Executive Council to clarify any situation which has been considered ambiguous or has given rise to a concern about its possible non-compliance with this Convention. The Executive Council shall respond by providing such assistance as appropriate.

6.   The Executive Council shall inform the States Parties about any request for clarification provided in this Article.

7.   If the doubt or concern of a State Party about a possible non-compliance has not been resolved within 60 days after the submission of the request for clarification to the Executive Council, or it believes its doubts warrant urgent consideration, notwithstanding its right to request a challenge inspection, it may request a special session of the Conference in accordance with Article VIII, paragraph 12 (*c*). At such a special session, the Conference shall consider the matter and may recommend any measure it deems appropriate to resolve the situation.

Procedures for challenge inspections

8. Each State Party has the right to request an on-site challenge inspection of any facility or location in the territory or in any other place under the jurisdiction or control of any other State Party for the sole purpose of clarifying and resolving any questions concerning possible non-compliance with the provisions of this Convention, and to have this inspection conducted anywhere without delay by an inspection team designated by the Director-General and in accordance with the Verification Annex.

9. Each State Party is under the obligation to keep the inspection request within the scope of this Convention and to provide in the inspection request all appropriate information on the basis of which a concern has arisen regarding possible non-compliance with this Convention as specified in the Verification Annex. Each State Party shall refrain from unfounded inspection requests, care being taken to avoid abuse. The challenge inspection shall be carried out for the sole purpose of determining facts relating to the possible non-compliance.

10. For the purpose of verifying compliance with the provisions of this Convention, each State Party shall permit the Technical Secretariat to conduct the on-site challenge inspection pursuant to paragraph 8.

11. Pursuant to a request for a challenge inspection of a facility or location, and in accordance with the procedures provided for in the Verification Annex, the inspected State Party shall have:

(*a*) The right and the obligation to make every reasonable effort to demonstrate its compliance with this Convention and, to this end, to enable the inspection team to fulfil its mandate;

(*b*) The obligation to provide access within the requested site for the sole purpose of establishing facts relevant to the concern regarding possible non-compliance; and

(*c*) The right to take measures to protect sensitive installations, and to prevent disclosure of confidential information and data, not related to this Convention.

12. With regard to an observer, the following shall apply:

(*a*) The requesting State Party may, subject to the agreement of the inspected State Party, send a representative who may be a national either of the requesting State Party or of a third State Party, to observe the conduct of the challenge inspection.

(*b*) The inspected State Party shall then grant access to the observer in accordance with the Verification Annex.

(*c*)   The inspected State Party shall, as a rule, accept the proposed observer, but if the inspected State Party exercises a refusal, that fact shall be recorded in the final report.

13.   The requesting State Party shall present an inspection request for an on-site challenge inspection to the Executive Council and at the same time to the Director-General for immediate processing.

14.   The Director-General shall immediately ascertain that the inspection request meets the requirements specified in Part X, paragraph 4, of the Verification Annex, and, if necessary, assist the requesting State Party in filing the inspection request accordingly. When the inspection request fulfils the requirements, preparations for the challenge inspection shall begin.

15.   The Director-General shall transmit the inspection request to the inspected State Party not less than 12 hours before the planned arrival of the inspection team at the point of entry.

16.   After having received the inspection request, the Executive Council shall take cognizance of the Director-General's actions on the request and shall keep the case under its consideration throughout the inspection procedure. However, its deliberations shall not delay the inspection process.

17.   The Executive Council may, not later than 12 hours after having received the inspection request, decide by a three-quarter majority of all its members against carrying out the challenge inspection, if it considers the inspection request to be frivolous, abusive or clearly beyond the scope of this Convention as described in paragraph 8. Neither the requesting nor the inspected State Party shall participate in such a decision. If the Executive Council decides against the challenge inspection, preparations shall be stopped, no further action on the inspection request shall be taken, and the States Parties concerned shall be informed accordingly.

18.   The Director-General shall issue an inspection mandate for the conduct of the challenge inspection. The inspection mandate shall be the inspection request referred to in paragraphs 8 and 9 put into operational terms, and shall conform with the inspection request.

19.   The challenge inspection shall be conducted in accordance with Part X or, in the case of alleged use, in accordance with Part XI of the Verification Annex. The inspection team shall be guided by the principle of conducting the challenge inspection in the least intrusive manner possible, consistent with the effective and timely accomplishment of its mission.

20.   The inspected State Party shall assist the inspection team throughout the challenge inspection and facilitate its task. If the inspected State Party proposes,

pursuant to Part X, Section C, of the Verification Annex, arrangements to demonstrate compliance with this Convention, alternative to full and comprehensive access, it shall make every reasonable effort, through consultations with the inspection team, to reach agreement on the modalities for establishing the facts with the aim of demonstrating its compliance.

21. The final report shall contain the factual findings as well as an assessment by the inspection team of the degree and nature of access and cooperation granted for the satisfactory implementation of the challenge inspection. The Director-General shall promptly transmit the final report of the inspection team to the requesting State Party, to the inspected State Party, to the Executive Council and to all other States Parties. The Director-General shall further transmit promptly to the Executive Council the assessments of the requesting and of the inspected States Parties, as well as the views of other States Parties which may be conveyed to the Director-General for that purpose, and then provide them to all States Parties.

22. The Executive Council shall, in accordance with its powers and functions, review the final report of the inspection team as soon as it is presented, and address any concerns as to:

(*a*)   Whether any non-compliance has occurred;

(*b*)   Whether the request had been within the scope of this Convention; and

(*c*)   Whether the right to request a challenge inspection had been abused.

23. If the Executive Council reaches the conclusion, in keeping with its powers and functions, that further action may be necessary with regard to paragraph 22, it shall take the appropriate measures to redress the situation and to ensure compliance with this Convention, including specific recommendations to the Conference. In the case of abuse, the Executive Council shall examine whether the requesting State Party should bear any of the financial implications of the challenge inspection.

24. The requesting State Party and the inspected State Party shall have the right to participate in the review process. The Executive Council shall inform the States Parties and the next session of the Conference of the outcome of the process.

25. If the Executive Council has made specific recommendations to the Conference, the Conference shall consider action in accordance with Article XII.

Article X

ASSISTANCE AND PROTECTION AGAINST CHEMICAL WEAPONS

1.   For the purposes of this Article, "Assistance" means the coordination and delivery to States Parties of protection against chemical weapons, including, *inter alia,* the following: detection equipment and alarm systems; protective equipment; decontamination equipment and decontaminants; medical antidotes and treatments; and advice on any of these protective measures.

2.   Nothing in this Convention shall be interpreted as impeding the right of any State Party to conduct research into, develop, produce, acquire, transfer or use means of protection against chemical weapons, for purposes not prohibited under this Convention.

3.   Each State Party undertakes to facilitate, and shall have the right to participate in, the fullest possible exchange of equipment, material and scientific and technological information concerning means of protection against chemical weapons.

4.   For the purposes of increasing the transparency of national programmes related to protective purposes, each State Party shall provide annually to the Technical Secretariat information on its programme, in accordance with procedures to be considered and approved by the Conference pursuant to Article VIII, paragraph 21 (*i*).

5.   The Technical Secretariat shall establish, not later than 180 days after entry into force of this Convention and maintain, for the use of any requesting State Party, a data bank containing freely available information concerning various means of protection against chemical weapons as well as such information as may be provided by States Parties.

The Technical Secretariat shall also, within the resources available to it, and at the request of a State Party, provide expert advice and assist the State Party in identifying how its programmes for the development and improvement of a protective capacity against chemical weapons could be implemented.

6.   Nothing in this Convention shall be interpreted as impeding the right of States Parties to request and provide assistance bilaterally and to conclude individual agreements with other States Parties concerning the emergency procurement of assistance.

7.   Each State Party undertakes to provide assistance through the Organization and to this end to elect to take one or more of the following measures:

(*a*)   To contribute to the voluntary fund for assistance to be established by the Conference at its first session;

(*b*)   To conclude, if possible not later than 180 days after this Convention enters into force for it, agreements with the Organization concerning the procurement, upon demand, of assistance;

(*c*)   To declare, not later than 180 days after this Convention enters into force for it, the kind of assistance it might provide in response to an appeal by the Organization. If, however, a State Party subsequently is unable to provide the assistance envisaged in its declaration, it is still under the obligation to provide assistance in accordance with this paragraph.

8.   Each State Party has the right to request and, subject to the procedures set forth in paragraphs 9, 10 and 11, to receive assistance and protection against the use or threat of use of chemical weapons if it considers that:

(*a*)   Chemical weapons have been used against it;

(*b*)   Riot control agents have been used against it as a method of warfare; or

(*c*)   It is threatened by actions or activities of any State that are prohibited for States Parties by Article I.

9.   The request, substantiated by relevant information, shall be submitted to the Director-General, who shall transmit it immediately to the Executive Council and to all States Parties. The Director-General shall immediately forward the request to States Parties which have volunteered, in accordance with paragraphs 7 (*b*) and (*c*), to dispatch emergency assistance in case of use of chemical weapons or use of riot control agents as a method of warfare, or humanitarian assistance in case of serious threat of use of chemical weapons or serious threat of use of riot control agents as a method of warfare to the State Party concerned not later than 12 hours after receipt of the request. The Director-General shall initiate, not later than 24 hours after receipt of the request, an investigation in order to provide foundation for further action. He shall complete the investigation within 72 hours and forward a report to the Executive Council. If additional time is required for completion of the investigation, an interim report shall be submitted within the same time-frame. The additional time required for investigation shall not exceed 72 hours. It may, however, be further extended by similar periods. Reports at the end of each additional period shall be submitted to the Executive Council. The investigation shall, as appropriate and in conformity with the request and the information accompanying the request, establish relevant facts related to the request as well as the type and scope of supplementary assistance and protection needed.

10. The Executive Council shall meet not later than 24 hours after receiving an investigation report to consider the situation and shall take a decision by simple

majority within the following 24 hours on whether to instruct the Technical Secretariat to provide supplementary assistance. The Technical Secretariat shall immediately transmit to all States Parties and relevant international organizations the investigation report and the decision taken by the Executive Council. When so decided by the Executive Council, the Director-General shall provide assistance immediately. For this purpose, the Director-General may cooperate with the requesting State Party, other States Parties and relevant international organizations. The States Parties shall make the fullest possible efforts to provide assistance.

11.   If the information available from the ongoing investigation or other reliable sources would give sufficient proof that there are victims of use of chemical weapons and immediate action is indispensable, the Director-General shall notify all States Parties and shall take emergency measures of assistance, using the resources the Conference has placed at his disposal for such contingencies. The Director-General shall keep the Executive Council informed of actions undertaken pursuant to this paragraph.

Article XI

ECONOMIC AND TECHNOLOGICAL DEVELOPMENT

1.   The provisions of this Convention shall be implemented in a manner which avoids hampering the economic or technological development of States Parties, and international cooperation in the field of chemical activities for purposes not prohibited under this Convention including the international exchange of scientific and technical information and chemicals and equipment for the production, processing or use of chemicals for purposes not prohibited under this Convention.

2.   Subject to the provisions of this Convention and without prejudice to the principles and applicable rules of international law, the States Parties shall:

(*a*)   Have the right, individually or collectively, to conduct research with, to develop, produce, acquire, retain, transfer, and use chemicals;

(*b*)   Undertake to facilitate, and have the right to participate in, the fullest possible exchange of chemicals, equipment and scientific and technical information relating to the development and application of chemistry for purposes not prohibited under this Convention;

(*c*)   Not maintain among themselves any restrictions, including those in any international agreements, incompatible with the obligations undertaken under this Convention, which would restrict or impede trade and the development and promotion of scientific and technological knowledge in the field of chemistry for industrial, agricultural, research, medical, pharmaceutical or other peaceful purposes;

(*d*)   Not use this Convention as grounds for applying any measures other than those provided for, or permitted, under this Convention nor use any other international agreement for pursuing an objective inconsistent with this Convention;

(*e*)   Undertake to review their existing national regulations in the field of trade in chemicals in order to render them consistent with the object and purpose of this Convention.

Article XII

Measures to redress a situation and to ensure compliance, including sanctions

1. The Conference shall take the necessary measures, as set forth in paragraphs 2, 3 and 4, to ensure compliance with this Convention and to redress and remedy any situation which contravenes the provisions of this Convention. In considering action pursuant to this paragraph, the Conference shall take into account all information and recommendations on the issues submitted by the Executive Council.

2. In cases where a State Party has been requested by the Executive Council to take measures to redress a situation raising problems with regard to its compliance, and where the State Party fails to fulfil the request within the specified time, the Conference may, *inter alia,* upon the recommendation of the Executive Council, restrict or suspend the State Party's rights and privileges under this Convention until it undertakes the necessary action to conform with its obligations under this Convention.

3. In cases where serious damage to the object and purpose of this Convention may result from activities prohibited under this Convention, in particular by Article I, the Conference may recommend collective measures to States Parties in conformity with international law.

4. The Conference shall, in cases of particular gravity, bring the issue, including relevant information and conclusions, to the attention of the United Nations General Assembly and the United Nations Security Council.

Article XIII

Relation to other international agreements

Nothing in this Convention shall be interpreted as in any way limiting or detracting from the obligations assumed by any State under the Protocol for the Prohibition of the Use in War of Asphyxiating, Poisonous or Other Gases, and of Bacteriological Methods of Warfare, signed at Geneva on 17 June 1925, and under the Convention on the Prohibition of the Development, Production and Stockpiling of Bacteriological (Biological) and Toxin Weapons and on Their Destruction, signed at London, Moscow and Washington on 10 April 1972.

Article XIV

SETTLEMENT OF DISPUTES

1.   Disputes that may arise concerning the application or the interpretation of this Convention shall be settled in accordance with the relevant provisions of this Convention and in conformity with the provisions of the Charter of the United Nations.

2.   When a dispute arises between two or more States Parties, or between one or more States Parties and the Organization, relating to the interpretation or application of this Convention, the parties concerned shall consult together with a view to the expeditious settlement of the dispute by negotiation or by other peaceful means of the parties' choice, including recourse to appropriate organs of this Convention and, by mutual consent, referral to the International Court of Justice in conformity with the Statute of the Court. The States Parties involved shall keep the Executive Council informed of actions being taken.

3.   The Executive Council may contribute to the settlement of a dispute by whatever means it deems appropriate, including offering its good offices, calling upon the States Parties to a dispute to start the settlement process of their choice and recommending a time-limit for any agreed procedure.

4.   The Conference shall consider questions related to disputes raised by States Parties or brought to its attention by the Executive Council. The Conference shall, as it finds necessary, establish or entrust organs with tasks related to the settlement of these disputes in conformity with Article VIII, paragraph 21 (*f*).

5.   The Conference and the Executive Council are separately empowered, subject to authorization from the General Assembly of the United Nations, to request the International Court of Justice to give an advisory opinion on any legal question arising within the scope of the activities of the Organization. An agreement between the Organization and the United Nations shall be concluded for this purpose in accordance with Article VIII, paragraph 34 (*a*).

6.   This Article is without prejudice to Article IX or to the provisions on measures to redress a situation and to ensure compliance, including sanctions.

Article XV

AMENDMENTS

1.   Any State Party may propose amendments to this Convention. Any State Party may also propose changes, as specified in paragraph 4, to the Annexes of this Convention. Proposals for amendments shall be subject to the procedures in paragraphs 2 and 3. Proposals for changes, as specified in paragraph 4, shall be subject to the procedures in paragraph 5.

2.   The text of a proposed amendment shall be submitted to the Director-General for circulation to all States Parties and to the Depositary. The proposed amendment shall be considered only by an Amendment Conference. Such an Amendment Conference shall be convened if one third or more of the States Parties notify the Director-General not later than 30 days after its circulation that they support further consideration of the proposal. The Amendment Conference shall be held immediately following a regular session of the Conference unless the requesting States Parties ask for an earlier meeting. In no case shall an Amendment Conference be held less than 60 days after the circulation of the proposed amendment.

3.   Amendments shall enter into force for all States Parties 30 days after deposit of the instruments of ratification or acceptance by all the States Parties referred to under subparagraph (*b*) below:

(*a*)   When adopted by the Amendment Conference by a positive vote of a majority of all States Parties with no State Party casting a negative vote; and

(*b*)   Ratified or accepted by all those States Parties casting a positive vote at the Amendment Conference.

4.   In order to ensure the viability and the effectiveness of this Convention, provisions in the Annexes shall be subject to changes in accordance with paragraph 5, if proposed changes are related only to matters of an administrative or technical nature. All changes to the Annex on Chemicals shall be made in accordance with paragraph 5. Sections A and C of the Confidentiality Annex, Part X of the Verification Annex, and those definitions in Part I of the Verification Annex which relate exclusively to challenge inspections, shall not be subject to changes in accordance with paragraph 5.

5.   Proposed changes referred to in paragraph 4 shall be made in accordance with the following procedures:

(*a*)   The text of the proposed changes shall be transmitted together with the necessary information to the Director-General. Additional information for the evaluation of the proposal may be provided by any State Party and the Director-General. The Director-General shall promptly communicate any such proposals and information to all States Parties, the Executive Council and the Depositary;

(b)   Not later than 60 days after its receipt, the Director-General shall evaluate the proposal to determine all its possible consequences for the provisions of this Convention and its implementation and shall communicate any such information to all States Parties and the Executive Council;

(c)   The Executive Council shall examine the proposal in the light of all information available to it, including whether the proposal fulfils the requirements of paragraph 4. Not later than 90 days after its receipt, the Executive Council shall notify its recommendation, with appropriate explanations, to all States Parties for consideration. States Parties shall acknowledge receipt within 10 days;

(d)   If the Executive Council recommends to all States Parties that the proposal be adopted, it shall be considered approved if no State Party objects to it within 90 days after receipt of the recommendation. If the Executive Council recommends that the proposal be rejected, it shall be considered rejected if no State Party objects to the rejection within 90 days after receipt of the recommendation;

(e)   If a recommendation of the Executive Council does not meet with the acceptance required under subparagraph (d), a decision on the proposal, including whether it fulfils the requirements of paragraph 4, shall be taken as a matter of substance by the Conference at its next session;

(f)   The Director-General shall notify all States Parties and the Depositary of any decision under this paragraph;

(g)   Changes approved under this procedure shall enter into force for all States Parties 180 days after the date of notification by the Director-General of their approval unless another time period is recommended by the Executive Council or decided by the Conference.

Article XVI

DURATION AND WITHDRAWAL

1.   This Convention shall be of unlimited duration.

2.   Each State Party shall, in exercising its national sovereignty, have the right to withdraw from this Convention if it decides that extraordinary events, related to the subject-matter of this Convention, have jeopardized the supreme interests of its country. It shall give notice of such withdrawal 90 days in advance to all other States Parties, the Executive Council, the Depositary and the United Nations Security Council. Such notice shall include a statement of the extraordinary events it regards as having jeopardized its supreme interests.

3.   The withdrawal of a State Party from this Convention shall not in any way affect the duty of States to continue fulfilling the obligations assumed under any relevant rules of international law, particularly the Geneva Protocol of 1925.

Article XVII

STATUS OF THE ANNEXES

The Annexes form an integral part of this Convention. Any reference to this Convention includes the Annexes.

Article XVIII

SIGNATURE

This Convention shall be open for signature for all States before its entry into force.

Article XIX

RATIFICATION

This Convention shall be subject to ratification by States Signatories according to their respective constitutional processes.

Article XX

ACCESSION

Any State which does not sign this Convention before its entry into force may accede to it at any time thereafter.

Article XXI

ENTRY INTO FORCE

1.   This Convention shall enter into force 180 days after the date of the deposit of the 65th instrument of ratification, but in no case earlier than two years after its opening for signature.

2.   For States whose instruments of ratification or accession are deposited subsequent to the entry into force of this Convention, it shall enter into force on the 30th day following the date of deposit of their instrument of ratification or accession.

Article XXII

RESERVATIONS

The Articles of this Convention shall not be subject to reservations. The Annexes of this Convention shall not be subject to reservations incompatible with its object and purpose.

Article XXIII

DEPOSITARY

The Secretary-General of the United Nations is hereby designated as the Depositary of this Convention and shall, *inter alia:*

(*a*)   Promptly inform all signatory and acceding States of the date of each signature, the date of deposit of each instrument of ratification or accession and the date of the entry into force of this Convention, and of the receipt of other notices;

(*b*)   Transmit duly certified copies of this Convention to the Governments of all signatory and acceding States; and

(*c*)   Register this Convention pursuant to Article 102 of the Charter of the United Nations.

Article XXIV

AUTHENTIC TEXTS

This Convention, of which the Arabic, Chinese, English, French, Russian and Spanish texts are equally authentic, shall be deposited with the Secretary-General of the United Nations.

IN WITNESS WHEREOF the undersigned, being duly authorized to that effect, have signed this Convention.

DONE at Paris on the thirteenth day of January, one thousand nine hundred and ninety-three.

ANNEX ON CHEMICALS

CONTENTS

A. GUIDELINES FOR SCHEDULES OF CHEMICALS

Guidelines for Schedule 1

1. The following criteria shall be taken into account in considering whether a toxic chemical or precursor should be included in Schedule 1:

(*a*) It has been developed, produced, stockpiled or used as a chemical weapon as defined in Article II;

(*b*) It poses otherwise a high risk to the object and purpose of this Convention by virtue of its high potential for use in activities prohibited under this Convention because one or more of the following conditions are met:

(i) It possesses a chemical structure closely related to that of other toxic chemicals listed in Schedule 1, and has, or can be expected to have, comparable properties;

(ii) It possesses such lethal or incapacitating toxicity as well as other properties that would enable it to be used as a chemical weapon;

(iii) It may be used as a precursor in the final single technological stage of production of a toxic chemical listed in Schedule 1, regardless of whether this stage takes place in facilities, in munitions or elsewhere;

(*c*) It has little or no use for purposes not prohibited under this Convention.

Guidelines for Schedule 2

2. The following criteria shall be taken into account in considering whether a toxic chemical not listed in Schedule 1 or a precursor to a Schedule 1 chemical or to a chemical listed in Schedule 2, part A, should be included in Schedule 2:

(*a*) It poses a significant risk to the object and purpose of this Convention because it possesses such lethal or incapacitating toxicity as well as other properties that could enable it to be used as a chemical weapon;

(*b*) It may be used as a precursor in one of the chemical reactions at the final stage of formation of a chemical listed in Schedule 1 or Schedule 2, part A;

(*c*) It poses a significant risk to the object and purpose of this Convention by virtue of its importance in the production of a chemical listed in Schedule 1 or Schedule 2, part A;

(*d*) It is not produced in large commercial quantities for purposes not prohibited under this Convention.

Guidelines for Schedule 3

3. The following criteria shall be taken into account in considering whether a toxic chemical or precursor, not listed in other Schedules, should be included in Schedule 3:

(*a*) It has been produced, stockpiled or used as a chemical weapon;

(*b*) It poses otherwise a risk to the object and purpose of this Convention because it possesses such lethal or incapacitating toxicity as well as other properties that might enable it to be used as a chemical weapon;

(*c*) It poses a risk to the object and purpose of this Convention by virtue of its importance in the production of one or more chemicals listed in Schedule 1 or Schedule 2, part B;

(*d*) It may be produced in large commercial quantities for purposes not prohibited under this Convention.

B.   SCHEDULES OF CHEMICALS

The following Schedules list toxic chemicals and their precursors. For the purpose of implementing this Convention, these Schedules identify chemicals for the application of verification measures according to the provisions of the Verification Annex. Pursuant to Article II, subparagraph 1 (*a*), these Schedules do not constitute a definition of chemical weapons.

(Whenever reference is made to groups of dialkylated chemicals, followed by a list of alkyl groups in parentheses, all chemicals possible by all possible combinations of alkyl groups listed in the parentheses are considered as listed in the respective Schedule as long as they are not explicitly exempted. A chemical marked "*" on Schedule 2, part A, is subject to special thresholds for declaration and verification, as specified in Part VII of the Verification Annex.)

Schedule 1

(CAS registry number)

A.   Toxic chemicals:

(1)   O-Alkyl ($\leq C_{10}$, incl. cycloalkyl) alkyl
(Me, Et, n-Pr or i-Pr)-phosphonofluoridates

    e.g. Sarin: O-Isopropyl methylphosphonofluoridate   (107-44-8)
         Soman: O-Pinacolyl methylphosphonofluoridate   (96-64-0)

(2)   O-Alkyl ($\leq C_{10}$, incl. cycloalkyl) N,N-dialkyl
(Me, Et, n-Pr or i-Pr) phosphoramidocyanidates

    e.g. Tabun: O-Ethyl N,N-dimethyl
               phosphoramidocyanidate   (77-81-6)

(3)   O-Alkyl (H or $\leq C_{10}$, incl. cycloalkyl) S-2-dialkyl
(Me, Et, n-Pr or i-Pr)-aminoethyl alkyl
(Me, Et, n-Pr or i-Pr) phosphonothiolates and
corresponding alkylated or protonated salts

    e.g. VX: O-Ethyl S-2-diisopropylaminoethyl
           methyl phosphonothiolate   (50782-69-9)

(4)   Sulfur mustards:

2-Chloroethylchloromethylsulfide	(2625-76-5)
Mustard gas: Bis(2-chloroethyl)sulfide	(505-60-2)
Bis(2-chloroethylthio)methane	(63869-13-6)
Sesquimustard: 1,2-Bis(2-chloroethylthio)ethane	(3563-36-8)
1,3-Bis(2-chloroethylthio)-n-propane	(63905-10-2)
1,4-Bis(2-chloroethylthio)-n-butane	(142868-93-7)
1,5-Bis(2-chloroethylthio)-n-pentane	(142868-94-8)
Bis(2-chloroethylthiomethyl)ether	(63918-90-1)
O-Mustard: Bis(2-chloroethylthioethyl)ether	(63918-89-8)

(5)   Lewisites:

Lewisite 1: 2-Chlorovinyldichloroarsine	(541-25-3)
Lewisite 2: Bis(2-chlorovinyl)chloroarsine	(40334-69-8)
Lewisite 3: Tris(2-chlorovinyl)arsine	(40334-70-1)

(6)   Nitrogen mustards:

HN1: Bis(2-chloroethyl)ethylamine	(538-07-8)
HN2: Bis(2-chloroethyl)methylamine	(51-75-2)
HN3: Tris(2-chloroethyl)amine	(555-77-1)

(7)   Saxitoxin   (35523-89-8)

(8)   Ricin   (9009-86-3)

B.   Precursors:

(9)   Alkyl (Me, Et, n-Pr or i-Pr) phosphonyldifluorides

     e.g. DF: Methylphosphonyldifluoride   (676-99-3)

(10) O-Alkyl (H or $\leq C_{10}$, incl. cycloalkyl) O-2-dialkyl
(Me, Et, n-Pr or i-Pr)-aminoethyl alkyl
(Me, Et, n-Pr or i-Pr) phosphonites and
corresponding alkylated or protonated salts

     e.g. QL: O-Ethyl O-2-diisopropylaminoethyl
                 methylphosphonite   (57856-11-8)

(11) Chlorosarin: O-Isopropyl methylphosphonochloridate   (1445-76-7)

(12) Chlorosoman: O-Pinacolyl methylphosphonochloridate   (7040-57-5)

Schedule 2

A. Toxic chemicals:

(1) Amiton: O,O-Diethyl S-[2-(diethylamino)ethyl]
     phosphorothiolate
     and corresponding alkylated or protonated salts   (78-53-5)

(2) PFIB: 1,1,3,3,3-Pentafluoro-2-(trifluoromethyl)-
     1-propene   (382-21-8)

(3) BZ: 3-Quinuclidinyl benzilate (*)   (6581-06-2)

B. Precursors:

(4) Chemicals, except for those listed in Schedule 1,
     containing a phosphorus atom to which is bonded
     one methyl, ethyl or propyl (normal or iso) group
     but not further carbon atoms,

     e.g. Methylphosphonyl dichloride   (676-97-1)
           Dimethyl methylphosphonate   (756-79-6)

     Exemption: Fonofos: O-Ethyl S-phenyl
                           ethylphosphonothiolothionate   (944-22-9)

(5) N,N-Dialkyl (Me, Et, n-Pr or i-Pr) phosphoramidic
     dihalides

(6) Dialkyl (Me, Et, n-Pr or i-Pr) N,N-dialkyl
     (Me, Et, n-Pr or i-Pr)-phosphoramidates

(7) Arsenic trichloride   (7784-34-1)

(8) 2,2-Diphenyl-2-hydroxyacetic acid   (76-93-7)

(9) Quinuclidin-3-ol   (1619-34-7)

(10) N,N-Dialkyl (Me, Et, n-Pr or i-Pr) aminoethyl-2-
     chlorides and corresponding protonated salts

(11) N,N-Dialkyl (Me, Et, n-Pr or i-Pr) aminoethane-2-ols
     and corresponding protonated salts

     Exemptions: N,N-Dimethylaminoethanol   (108-01-0)
                    and corresponding protonated salts
                  N,N-Diethylaminoethanol   (100-37-8)
                    and corresponding protonated salts

(12) N,N-Dialkyl (Me, Et, n-Pr or i-Pr) aminoethane-2-thiols and corresponding protonated salts

(13) Thiodiglycol: Bis(2-hydroxyethyl)sulfide (111-48-8)

(14) Pinacolyl alcohol: 3,3-Dimethylbutan-2-ol (464-07-3)

Schedule 3

A. Toxic chemicals:

(1) Phosgene: Carbonyl dichloride (75-44-5)

(2) Cyanogen chloride (506-77-4)

(3) Hydrogen cyanide (74-90-8)

(4) Chloropicrin: Trichloronitromethane (76-06-2)

B. Precursors:

(5) Phosphorus oxychloride (10025-87-3)

(6) Phosphorus trichloride (7719-12-2)

(7) Phosphorus pentachloride (10026-13-8)

(8) Trimethyl phosphite (121-45-9)

(9) Triethyl phosphite (122-52-1)

(10) Dimethyl phosphite (868-85-9)

(11) Diethyl phosphite (762-04-9)

(12) Sulfur monochloride (10025-67-9)

(13) Sulfur dichloride (10545-99-0)

(14) Thionyl chloride (7719-09-7)

(15) Ethyldiethanolamine (139-87-7)

(16) Methyldiethanolamine (105-59-9)

(17) Triethanolamine (102-71-6)

ANNEX ON IMPLEMENTATION AND VERIFICATION
("VERIFICATION ANNEX")
CONTENTS

PART I

DEFINITIONS

1.   "Approved Equipment" means the devices and instruments necessary for the performance of the inspection team's duties that have been certified by the Technical Secretariat in accordance with regulations prepared by the Technical Secretariat pursuant to Part II, paragraph 27 of this Annex. Such equipment may also refer to the administrative supplies or recording materials that would be used by the inspection team.

2.   "Building" as referred to in the definition of chemical weapons production facility in Article II comprises specialized buildings and standard buildings.

(*a*)   "Specialized Building" means:

   (i)   Any building, including underground structures, containing specialized equipment in a production or filling configuration;

   (ii)   Any building, including underground structures, which has distinctive features which distinguish it from buildings normally used for chemical production or filling activities not prohibited under this Convention.

(*b*)   "Standard Building" means any building, including underground structures, constructed to prevailing industry standards for facilities not producing any chemical specified in Article II, paragraph 8 (*a*) (i), or corrosive chemicals.

3.   "Challenge Inspection" means the inspection of any facility or location in the territory or in any other place under the jurisdiction or control of a State Party requested by another State Party pursuant to Article IX, paragraphs 8 to 25.

4.   "Discrete Organic Chemical" means any chemical belonging to the class of chemical compounds consisting of all compounds of carbon except for its oxides, sulfides and metal carbonates, identifiable by chemical name, by structural formula, if known, and by Chemical Abstracts Service registry number, if assigned.

5.   "Equipment" as referred to in the definition of chemical weapons production facility in Article II comprises specialized equipment and standard equipment.

(*a*)   "Specialized Equipment" means:

(i)   The main production train, including any reactor or equipment for product synthesis, separation or purification, any equipment used directly for heat transfer in the final technological stage, such as in reactors or in product separation, as well as any other equipment which has been in contact with any chemical specified in Article II, paragraph 8 (*a*) (i), or would be in contact with such a chemical if the facility were operated;

(ii)   Any chemical weapon filling machines;

(iii)   Any other equipment specially designed, built or installed for the operation of the facility as a chemical weapons production facility, as distinct from a facility constructed according to prevailing commercial industry standards for facilities not producing any chemical specified in Article II, paragraph 8 (*a*) (i), or corrosive chemicals, such as: equipment made of high-nickel alloys or other special corrosion-resistant material; special equipment for waste control, waste treatment, air filtering, or solvent recovery; special containment enclosures and safety shields; non-standard laboratory equipment used to analyse toxic chemicals for chemical weapons purposes; custom-designed process control panels; or dedicated spares for specialized equipment.

(*b*) "Standard Equipment" means:

(i)   Production equipment which is generally used in the chemical industry and is not included in the types of specialized equipment;

(ii)   Other equipment commonly used in the chemical industry, such as: fire-fighting equipment; guard and security/safety surveillance equipment; medical facilities, laboratory facilities; or communications equipment.

6.   "Facility" in the context of Article VI means any of the industrial sites as defined below ("plant site","plant" and "unit").

(*a*) "Plant Site" (Works, Factory) means the local integration of one or more plants, with any intermediate administrative levels, which are under one operational control, and includes common infrastructure, such as:

(i)   Administration and other offices;

(ii) Repair and maintenance shops;

(iii) Medical centre;

(iv) Utilities;

(v)   Central analytical laboratory;

(vi) Research and development laboratories;

(vii) Central effluent and waste treatment area; and

(viii) Warehouse storage.

(b) "Plant" (Production facility, Workshop) means a relatively self-contained area, structure or building containing one or more units with auxiliary and associated infrastructure, such as:

(i)   Small administrative section;

(ii) Storage/handling areas for feedstock and products;

(iii) Effluent/waste handling/treatment area;

(iv) Control/analytical laboratory;

(v)   First aid service/related medical section; and

(vi) Records associated with the movement into, around and from the site, of declared chemicals and their feedstock or product chemicals formed from them, as appropriate.

(c) "Unit" (Production unit, Process unit) means the combination of those items of equipment, including vessels and vessel set up, necessary for the production, processing or consumption of a chemical.

7.   "Facility Agreement" means an agreement or arrangement between a State Party and the Organization relating to a specific facility subject to on-site verification pursuant to Articles IV, V and VI.

8.   "Host State" means the State on whose territory lie facilities or areas of another State, Party to this Convention, which are subject to inspection under this Convention.

9.   "In-Country Escort" means individuals specified by the inspected State Party and, if appropriate, by the Host State, if they so wish, to accompany and assist the inspection team during the in-country period.

10. "In-Country Period" means the period from the arrival of the inspection team at a point of entry until its departure from the State at a point of entry.

11. "Initial Inspection" means the first on-site inspection of facilities to verify declarations submitted pursuant to Articles III, IV, V and VI and this Annex.

12. "Inspected State Party" means the State Party on whose territory or in any other place under its jurisdiction or control an inspection pursuant to this Convention takes place, or the State Party whose facility or area on the territory of a Host State is subject to such an inspection; it does not, however, include the State Party specified in Part II, paragraph 21 of this Annex.

13. "Inspection Assistant" means an individual designated by the Technical Secretariat as set forth in Part II, Section A, of this Annex to assist inspectors in an inspection or visit, such as medical, security and administrative personnel and interpreters.

14. "Inspection Mandate" means the instructions issued by the Director-General to the inspection team for the conduct of a particular inspection.

15. "Inspection Manual" means the compilation of additional procedures for the conduct of inspections developed by the Technical Secretariat.

16. "Inspection Site" means any facility or area at which an inspection is carried out and which is specifically defined in the respective facility agreement or inspection request or mandate or inspection request as expanded by the alternative or final perimeter.

17. "Inspection Team" means the group of inspectors and inspection assistants assigned by the Director-General to conduct a particular inspection.

18. "Inspector" means an individual designated by the Technical Secretariat according to the procedures as set forth in Part II, Section A, of this Annex, to carry out an inspection or visit in accordance with this Convention.

19. "Model Agreement" means a document specifying the general form and content for an agreement concluded between a State Party and the Organization for fulfilling the verification provisions specified in this Annex.

20. "Observer" means a representative of a requesting State Party or a third State Party to observe a challenge inspection.

21. "Perimeter" in case of challenge inspection means the external boundary of the inspection site, defined by either geographic coordinates or description on a map.

(*a*) "Requested Perimeter" means the inspection site perimeter as specified in conformity with Part X, paragraph 8, of this Annex;

(*b*) "Alternative Perimeter" means the inspection site perimeter as specified, alternatively to the requested perimeter, by the inspected State Party; it shall conform to the requirements specified in Part X, paragraph 17, of this Annex;

(*c*) "Final Perimeter" means the final inspection site perimeter as agreed in negotiations between the inspection team and the inspected State Party, in accordance with Part X, paragraphs 16 to 21, of this Annex;

(*d*) "Declared Perimeter" means the external boundary of the facility declared pursuant to Articles III, IV, V and VI.

22. "Period of Inspection", for the purposes of Article IX, means the period of time from provision of access to the inspection team to the inspection site until its departure from the inspection site, exclusive of time spent on briefings before and after the verification activities.

23. "Period of Inspection", for the purposes of Articles IV, V and VI, means the period of time from arrival of the inspection team at the inspection site until its departure from the inspection site, exclusive of time spent on briefings before and after the verification activities.

24. "Point of Entry"/"Point of Exit" means a location designated for the in-country arrival of inspection teams for inspections pursuant to this Convention or for their departure after completion of their mission.

25. "Requesting State Party" means a State Party which has requested a challenge inspection pursuant to Article IX.

26. "Tonne" means metric ton, i.e. 1,000 kg.

PART II

GENERAL RULES OF VERIFICATION

A. DESIGNATION OF INSPECTORS AND INSPECTION ASSISTANTS

1.   Not later than 30 days after entry into force of this Convention the Technical Secretariat shall communicate, in writing, to all States Parties the names, nationalities and ranks of the inspectors and inspection assistants proposed for designation, as well as a description of their qualifications and professional experiences.

2.   Each State Party shall immediately acknowledge receipt of the list of inspectors and inspection assistants, proposed for designation communicated to it. The State Party shall inform the Technical Secretariat in writing of its acceptance of each inspector and inspection assistant, not later than 30 days after acknowledgement of receipt of the list. Any inspector and inspection assistant included in this list shall be regarded as designated unless a State Party, not later than 30 days after acknowledgement of receipt of the list, declares its non-acceptance in writing. The State Party may include the reason for the objection.

In the case of non-acceptance, the proposed inspector or inspection assistant shall not undertake or participate in verification activities on the territory or in any other place under the jurisdiction or control of the State Party which has declared its non-acceptance. The Technical Secretariat shall, as necessary, submit further proposals in addition to the original list.

3.   Verification activities under this Convention shall only be performed by designated inspectors and inspection assistants.

4.   Subject to the provisions of paragraph 5, a State Party has the right at any time to object to an inspector or inspection assistant who has already been designated. It shall notify the Technical Secretariat of its objection in writing and may include the reason for the objection. Such objection shall come into effect 30 days after receipt by the Technical Secretariat. The Technical Secretariat shall immediately inform the State Party concerned of the withdrawal of the designation of the inspector or inspection assistant.

5.   A State Party that has been notified of an inspection shall not seek to have removed from the inspection team for that inspection any of the designated inspectors or inspection assistants named in the inspection team list.

6.   The number of inspectors or inspection assistants accepted by and designated to a State Party must be sufficient to allow for availability and rotation of appropriate numbers of inspectors and inspection assistants.

7.   If, in the opinion of the Director-General, the non-acceptance of proposed inspectors or inspection assistants impedes the designation of a sufficient number of inspectors or inspection assistants or otherwise hampers the effective fulfilment of the tasks of the Technical Secretariat, the Director-General shall refer the issue to the Executive Council.

8.   Whenever amendments to the above-mentioned lists of inspectors and inspection assistants are necessary or requested, replacement inspectors and inspection assistants shall be designated in the same manner as set forth with respect to the initial list.

9.   The members of the inspection team carrying out an inspection of a facility of a State Party located on the territory of another State Party shall be designated in accordance with the procedures set forth in this Annex as applied both to the inspected State Party and the Host State Party.

B.   Privileges and Immunities

10. Each State Party shall, not later than 30 days after acknowledgement of receipt of the list of inspectors and inspection assistants or of changes thereto, provide multiple entry/exit and/or transit visas and other such documents to enable each inspector or inspection assistant to enter and to remain on the territory of that State Party for the purpose of carrying out inspection activities. These documents shall be valid for at least two years after their provision to the Technical Secretariat.

11. To exercise their functions effectively, inspectors and inspection assistants shall be accorded privileges and immunities as set forth in subparagraphs (*a*) to (*i*). Privileges and immunities shall be granted to members of the inspection team for the sake of this Convention and not for the personal benefit of the individuals themselves. Such privileges and immunities shall be accorded to them for the entire period between arrival on and departure from the territory of the inspected State Party or Host State, and thereafter with respect to acts previously performed in the exercise of their official functions.

(*a*)   The members of the inspection team shall be accorded the inviolability enjoyed by diplomatic agents pursuant to Article 29 of the Vienna Convention on Diplomatic Relations of 18 April 1961.

(*b*)   The living quarters and office premises occupied by the inspection team carrying out inspection activities pursuant to this Convention shall be accorded the inviolability and protection accorded to the premises of diplomatic agents pursuant to Article 30, paragraph 1, of the Vienna Convention on Diplomatic Relations.

(c)   The papers and correspondence, including records, of the inspection team shall enjoy the inviolability accorded to all papers and correspondence of diplomatic agents pursuant to Article 30, paragraph 2, of the Vienna Convention on Diplomatic Relations. The inspection team shall have the right to use codes for their communications with the Technical Secretariat.

(d)   Samples and approved equipment carried by members of the inspection team shall be inviolable subject to provisions contained in this Convention and exempt from all customs duties. Hazardous samples shall be transported in accordance with relevant regulations.

(e)   The members of the inspection team shall be accorded the immunities accorded to diplomatic agents pursuant to Article 31, paragraphs 1, 2 and 3, of the Vienna Convention on Diplomatic Relations.

(f)   The members of the inspection team carrying out prescribed activities pursuant to this Convention shall be accorded the exemption from dues and taxes accorded to diplomatic agents pursuant to Article 34 of the Vienna Convention on Diplomatic Relations.

(g)   The members of the inspection team shall be permitted to bring into the territory of the inspected State Party or Host State Party, without payment of any customs duties or related charges, articles for personal use, with the exception of articles the import or export of which is prohibited by law or controlled by quarantine regulations.

(h)   The members of the inspection team shall be accorded the same currency and exchange facilities as are accorded to representatives of foreign Governments on temporary official missions.

(i)   The members of the inspection team shall not engage in any professional or commercial activity for personal profit on the territory of the inspected State Party or the Host State.

12. When transiting the territory of non-inspected States Parties, the members of the inspection team shall be accorded the privileges and immunities enjoyed by diplomatic agents pursuant to Article 40, paragraph 1, of the Vienna Convention on Diplomatic Relations. Papers and correspondence, including records, and samples and approved equipment, carried by them, shall be accorded the privileges and immunities set forth in paragraph 11 (c) and (d).

13. Without prejudice to their privileges and immunities the members of the inspection team shall be obliged to respect the laws and regulations of the inspected State Party or Host State and, to the extent that is consistent with the inspection mandate, shall be obliged not to interfere in the internal affairs of that State. If the inspected State Party or Host State Party considers that there has been an abuse of privileges and immunities specified in this Annex, consultations shall

be held between the State Party and the Director-General to determine whether such an abuse has occurred and, if so determined, to prevent a repetition of such an abuse.

14. The immunity from jurisdiction of members of the inspection team may be waived by the Director-General in those cases when the Director-General is of the opinion that immunity would impede the course of justice and that it can be waived without prejudice to the implementation of the provisions of this Convention. Waiver must always be express.

15. Observers shall be accorded the same privileges and immunities accorded to inspectors pursuant to this section, except for those accorded pursuant to paragraph 11 (*d*).

C. STANDING ARRANGEMENTS

Points of entry

16. Each State Party shall designate the points of entry and shall supply the required information to the Technical Secretariat not later than 30 days after this Convention enters into force for it. These points of entry shall be such that the inspection team can reach any inspection site from at least one point of entry within 12 hours. Locations of points of entry shall be provided to all States Parties by the Technical Secretariat.

17. Each State Party may change the points of entry by giving notice of such change to the Technical Secretariat. Changes shall become effective 30 days after the Technical Secretariat receives such notification to allow appropriate notification to all States Parties.

18. If the Technical Secretariat considers that there are insufficient points of entry for the timely conduct of inspections or that changes to the points of entry proposed by a State Party would hamper such timely conduct of inspections, it shall enter into consultations with the State Party concerned to resolve the problem.

19. In cases where facilities or areas of an inspected State Party are located on the territory of a Host State Party or where the access from the point of entry to the facilities or areas subject to inspection requires transit through the territory of another State Party, the inspected State Party shall exercise the rights and fulfil the obligations concerning such inspections in accordance with this Annex. The Host State Party shall facilitate the inspection of those facilities or areas and shall provide for the necessary support to enable the inspection team to carry out its tasks in a timely and effective manner. States Parties through whose territory transit is required to inspect facilities or areas of an inspected State Party shall facilitate such transit.

20. In cases where facilities or areas of an inspected State Party are located on the territory of a State not Party to this Convention, the inspected State Party shall take all necessary measures to ensure that inspections of those facilities or areas can be carried out in accordance with the provisions of this Annex. A State Party that has one or more facilities or areas on the territory of a State not Party to this Convention shall take all necessary measures to ensure acceptance by the Host State of inspectors and inspection assistants designated to that State Party. If an inspected State Party is unable to ensure access, it shall demonstrate that it took all necessary measures to ensure access.

21. In cases where the facilities or areas sought to be inspected are located on the territory of a State Party, but in a place under the jurisdiction or control of a State not Party to this Convention, the State Party shall take all necessary measures as would be required of an inspected State Party and a Host State Party to ensure that inspections of such facilities or areas can be carried out in accordance with the provisions of this Annex. If the State Party is unable to ensure access to those facilities or areas, it shall demonstrate that it took all necessary measures to ensure access. This paragraph shall not apply where the facilities or areas sought to be inspected are those of the State Party.

Arrangements for use of non-scheduled aircraft

22. For inspections pursuant to Article IX and for other inspections where timely travel is not feasible using scheduled commercial transport, an inspection team may need to utilize aircraft owned or chartered by the Technical Secretariat. Not later than 30 days after this Convention enters into force for it, each State Party shall inform the Technical Secretariat of the standing diplomatic clearance number for non-scheduled aircraft transporting inspection teams and equipment necessary for inspection into and out of the territory in which an inspection site is located. Aircraft routings to and from the designated point of entry shall be along established international airways that are agreed upon between the States Parties and the Technical Secretariat as the basis for such diplomatic clearance.

23. When a non-scheduled aircraft is used, the Technical Secretariat shall provide the inspected State Party with a flight plan, through the National Authority, for the aircraft's flight from the last airfield prior to entering the airspace of the State in which the inspection site is located to the point of entry, not less than six hours before the scheduled departure time from that airfield. Such a plan shall be filed in accordance with the procedures of the International Civil Aviation Organization applicable to civil aircraft. For its owned or chartered flights, the Technical Secretariat shall include in the remarks section of each flight plan the standing diplomatic clearance number and the appropriate notation identifying the aircraft as an inspection aircraft.

24. Not less than three hours before the scheduled departure of the inspection team from the last airfield prior to entering the airspace of the State in which the inspection is to take place, the inspected State Party or Host State Party shall ensure that the flight plan filed in accordance with paragraph 23 is approved so that the inspection team may arrive at the point of entry by the estimated arrival time.

25. The inspected State Party shall provide parking, security protection, servicing and fuel as required by the Technical Secretariat for the aircraft of the inspection team at the point of entry when such aircraft is owned or chartered by the Technical Secretariat. Such aircraft shall not be liable for landing fees, departure tax, and similar charges. The Technical Secretariat shall bear the cost of such fuel, security protection and servicing.

Administrative arrangements

26. The inspected State Party shall provide or arrange for the amenities necessary for the inspection team such as communication means, interpretation services to the extent necessary for the performance of interviewing and other tasks, transportation, working space, lodging, meals and medical care. In this regard, the inspected State Party shall be reimbursed by the Organization for such costs incurred by the inspection team.

Approved equipment

27. Subject to paragraph 29, there shall be no restriction by the inspected State Party on the inspection team bringing onto the inspection site such equipment, approved in accordance with paragraph 28, which the Technical Secretariat has determined to be necessary to fulfil the inspection requirements. The Technical Secretariat shall prepare and, as appropriate, update a list of approved equipment, which may be needed for the purposes described above, and regulations governing such equipment which shall be in accordance with this Annex. In establishing the list of approved equipment and these regulations, the Technical Secretariat shall ensure that safety considerations for all the types of facilities at which such equipment is likely to be used, are taken fully into account. A list of approved equipment shall be considered and approved by the Conference pursuant to Article VIII, paragraph 21 (*i*).

28. The equipment shall be in the custody of the Technical Secretariat and be designated, calibrated and approved by the Technical Secretariat. The Technical Secretariat shall, to the extent possible, select that equipment which is specifically designed for the specific kind of inspection required. Designated and approved equipment shall be specifically protected against unauthorized alteration.

29. The inspected State Party shall have the right, without prejudice to the prescribed time-frames, to inspect the equipment in the presence of inspection team members at the point of entry, i.e., to check the identity of the equipment brought in or removed from the territory of the inspected State Party or the Host State. To facilitate such identification, the Technical Secretariat shall attach documents and devices to authenticate its designation and approval of the equipment. The inspection of the equipment shall also ascertain to the satisfaction of the inspected State Party that the equipment meets the description of the approved equipment for the particular type of inspection. The inspected State Party may exclude equipment not meeting that description or equipment without the above-mentioned authentication documents and devices. Procedures for the inspection of equipment shall be considered and approved by the Conference pursuant to Article VIII, paragraph 21 (*i*).

30. In cases where the inspection team finds it necessary to use equipment available on site not belonging to the Technical Secretariat and requests the inspected State Party to enable the team to use such equipment, the inspected State Party shall comply with the request to the extent it can.

D. PRE-INSPECTION ACTIVITIES

Notification

31. The Director-General shall notify the State Party before the planned arrival of the inspection team at the point of entry and within the prescribed time-frames, where specified, of its intention to carry out an inspection.

32. Notifications made by the Director-General shall include the following information:

(*a*) The type of inspection;

(*b*) The point of entry;

(*c*) The date and estimated time of arrival at the point of entry;

(*d*) The means of arrival at the point of entry;

(*e*) The site to be inspected;

(*f*) The names of inspectors and inspection assistants;

(*g*) If appropriate, aircraft clearance for special flights.

33. The inspected State Party shall acknowledge the receipt of a notification by the Technical Secretariat of an intention to conduct an inspection, not later than one hour after receipt of such notification.

34. In the case of an inspection of a facility of a State Party located on the territory of another State Party, both States Parties shall be simultaneously notified in accordance with paragraphs 31 and 32.

Entry into the territory of the inspected State Party or Host State and transfer to the inspection site

35. The inspected State Party or Host State Party which has been notified of the arrival of an inspection team, shall ensure its immediate entry into the territory and shall through an in-country escort or by other means do everything in its power to ensure the safe conduct of the inspection team and its equipment and supplies, from its point of entry to the inspection site(s) and to a point of exit.

36. The inspected State Party or Host State Party shall, as necessary, assist the inspection team in reaching the inspection site not later than 12 hours after the arrival at the point of entry.

Pre-inspection briefing

37. Upon arrival at the inspection site and before the commencement of the inspection, the inspection team shall be briefed by facility representatives, with the aid of maps and other documentation as appropriate, on the facility, the activities carried out there, safety measures and administrative and logistic arrangements necessary for the inspection. The time spent for the briefing shall be limited to the minimum necessary and in any event not exceed three hours.

E.   CONDUCT OF INSPECTIONS

General rules

38. The members of the inspection team shall discharge their functions in accordance with the provisions of this Convention, as well as rules established by the Director-General and facility agreements concluded between States Parties and the Organization.

39. The inspection team shall strictly observe the inspection mandate issued by the Director-General. It shall refrain from activities going beyond this mandate.

40. The activities of the inspection team shall be so arranged as to ensure the timely and effective discharge of its functions and the least possible inconvenience to the inspected State Party or Host State and disturbance to the facility or area inspected. The inspection team shall avoid unnecessarily hampering or delaying the operation of a facility and avoid affecting its safety.

In particular, the inspection team shall not operate any facility. If inspectors consider that, to fulfil their mandate, particular operations should be carried out in a facility, they shall request the designated representative of the inspected facility to have them performed. The representative shall carry out the request to the extent possible.

41. In the performance of their duties on the territory of an inspected State Party or Host State, the members of the inspection team shall, if the inspected State Party so requests, be accompanied by representatives of the inspected State Party, but the inspection team must not thereby be delayed or otherwise hindered in the exercise of its functions.

42. Detailed procedures for the conduct of inspections shall be developed for inclusion in the inspection manual by the Technical Secretariat, taking into account guidelines to be considered and approved by the Conference pursuant to Article VIII, paragraph 21 (*i*).

Safety

43. In carrying out their activities, inspectors and inspection assistants shall observe safety regulations established at the inspection site, including those for the protection of controlled environments within a facility and for personal safety. In order to implement these requirements, appropriate detailed procedures shall be considered and approved by the Conference pursuant to Article VIII, paragraph 21 (*i*).

Communications

44. Inspectors shall have the right throughout the in-country period to communicate with the Headquarters of the Technical Secretariat. For this purpose they may use their own, duly certified, approved equipment and may request that the inspected State Party or Host State Party provide them with access to other telecommunications. The inspection team shall have the right to use its own two-way system of radio communications between personnel patrolling the perimeter and other members of the inspection team.

Inspection team and inspected State Party rights

45. The inspection team shall, in accordance with the relevant Articles and Annexes of this Convention as well as with facility agreements and procedures set forth in the inspection manual, have the right to unimpeded access to the inspection site. The items to be inspected will be chosen by the inspectors.

46. Inspectors shall have the right to interview any facility personnel in the presence of representatives of the inspected State Party with the

purpose of establishing relevant facts. Inspectors shall only request information and data which are necessary for the conduct of the inspection, and the inspected State Party shall furnish such information upon request. The inspected State Party shall have the right to object to questions posed to the facility personnel if those questions are deemed not relevant to the inspection. If the head of the inspection team objects and states their relevance, the questions shall be provided in writing to the inspected State Party for reply. The inspection team may note any refusal to permit interviews or to allow questions to be answered and any explanations given, in that part of the inspection report that deals with the cooperation of the inspected State Party.

47.   Inspectors shall have the right to inspect documentation and records they deem relevant to the conduct of their mission.

48.   Inspectors shall have the right to have photographs taken at their request by representatives of the inspected State Party or of the inspected facility. The capability to take instant development photographic prints shall be available. The inspection team shall determine whether photographs conform to those requested and, if not, repeat photographs shall be taken. The inspection team and the inspected State Party shall each retain one copy of every photograph.

49.   The representatives of the inspected State Party shall have the right to observe all verification activities carried out by the inspection team.

50.   The inspected State Party shall receive copies, at its request, of the information and data gathered about its facility(ies) by the Technical Secretariat.

51.   Inspectors shall have the right to request clarifications in connection with ambiguities that arise during an inspection. Such requests shall be made promptly through the representative of the inspected State Party. The representative of the inspected State Party shall provide the inspection team, during the inspection, with such clarification as may be necessary to remove the ambiguity. If questions relating to an object or a building located within the inspection site are not resolved, the object or building shall, if requested, be photographed for the purpose of clarifying its nature and function. If the ambiguity cannot be removed during the inspection, the inspectors shall notify the Technical Secretariat immediately. The inspectors shall include in the inspection report any such unresolved question, relevant clarifications, and a copy of any photographs taken.

Collection, handling and analysis of samples

52.   Representatives of the inspected State Party or of the inspected facility shall take samples at the request of the inspection team in the presence of inspectors. If so agreed in advance with the representatives of the inspected State Party or of the inspected facility, the inspection team may take samples itself.

53. Where possible, the analysis of samples shall be performed on-site. The inspection team shall have the right to perform on-site analysis of samples using approved equipment brought by it. At the request of the inspection team, the inspected State Party shall, in accordance with agreed procedures, provide assistance for the analysis of samples on-site. Alternatively, the inspection team may request that appropriate analysis on-site be performed in its presence.

54. The inspected State Party has the right to retain portions of all samples taken or take duplicate samples and be present when samples are analysed on-site.

55. The inspection team shall, if it deems it necessary, transfer samples for analysis off-site at laboratories designated by the Organization.

56. The Director-General shall have the primary responsibility for the security, integrity and preservation of samples and for ensuring that the confidentiality of samples transferred for analysis off-site is protected. The Director-General shall do so in accordance with procedures, to be considered and approved by the Conference pursuant to Article VIII, paragraph 21 (*i*), for inclusion in the inspection manual. He shall:

(*a*)   Establish a stringent regime governing the collection, handling, transport and analysis of samples;

(*b*)   Certify the laboratories designated to perform different types of analysis;

(*c*)   Oversee the standardization of equipment and procedures at these designated laboratories, mobile analytical equipment and procedures, and monitor quality control and overall standards in relation to the certification of these laboratories, mobile equipment and procedures; and

(*d*)   Select from among the designated laboratories those which shall perform analytical or other functions in relation to specific investigations.

57. When off-site analysis is to be performed, samples shall be analysed in at least two designated laboratories. The Technical Secretariat shall ensure the expeditious processing of the analysis. The samples shall be accounted for by the Technical Secretariat and any unused samples or portions thereof shall be returned to the Technical Secretariat.

58. The Technical Secretariat shall compile the results of the laboratory analysis of samples relevant to compliance with this Convention and include them in the final inspection report. The Technical Secretariat shall include in the report

detailed information concerning the equipment and methodology employed by the designated laboratories.

Extension of inspection duration

59. Periods of inspection may be extended by agreement with the representative of the inspected State Party.

Debriefing

60. Upon completion of an inspection the inspection team shall meet with representatives of the inspected State Party and the personnel responsible for the inspection site to review the preliminary findings of the inspection team and to clarify any ambiguities. The inspection team shall provide to the representatives of the inspected State Party its preliminary findings in written form according to a standardized format, together with a list of any samples and copies of written information and data gathered and other material to be taken off-site. The document shall be signed by the head of the inspection team. In order to indicate that he has taken notice of the contents of the document, the representative of the inspected State Party shall countersign the document. This meeting shall be completed not later than 24 hours after the completion of the inspection.

F. DEPARTURE

61. Upon completion of the post-inspection procedures, the inspection team shall leave, as soon as possible, the territory of the inspected State Party or the Host State.

G. REPORTS

62. Not later than 10 days after the inspection, the inspectors shall prepare a factual, final report on the activities conducted by them and on their findings. It shall only contain facts relevant to compliance with this Convention, as provided for under the inspection mandate. The report shall also provide information as to the manner in which the State Party inspected cooperated with the inspection team. Differing observations made by inspectors may be attached to the report. The report shall be kept confidential.

63. The final report shall immediately be submitted to the inspected State Party. Any written comments, which the inspected State Party may immediately make on its findings shall be annexed to it. The final report together with annexed comments made by the inspected State Party shall be submitted to the Director-General not later than 30 days after the inspection.

64. Should the report contain uncertainties, or should cooperation between the National Authority and the inspectors not measure up to the standards required, the Director-General shall approach the State Party for clarification.

65. If the uncertainties cannot be removed or the facts established are of a nature to suggest that obligations undertaken under this Convention have not been met, the Director-General shall inform the Executive Council without delay.

H.   APPLICATION OF GENERAL PROVISIONS

66. The provisions of this Part shall apply to all inspections conducted pursuant to this Convention, except where the provisions of this Part differ from the provisions set forth for specific types of inspections in Parts III to XI of this Annex, in which case the latter provisions shall take precedence.

PART III

GENERAL PROVISIONS FOR VERIFICATION MEASURES PURSUANT TO
ARTICLES IV, V AND VI, PARAGRAPH 3

A.   INITIAL INSPECTIONS AND FACILITY AGREEMENTS

1.   Each declared facility subject to on-site inspection pursuant to Articles IV, V, and VI, paragraph 3, shall receive an initial inspection promptly after the facility is declared. The purpose of this inspection of the facility shall be to verify information provided and to obtain any additional information needed for planning future verification activities at the facility, including on-site inspections and continuous monitoring with on-site instruments, and to work on the facility agreements.

2.   States Parties shall ensure that the verification of declarations and the initiation of the systematic verification measures can be accomplished by the Technical Secretariat at all facilities within the established time-frames after this Convention enters into force for them.

3.   Each State Party shall conclude a facility agreement with the Organization for each facility declared and subject to on-site inspection pursuant to Articles IV, V, and VI, paragraph 3.

4.   Facility agreements shall be completed not later than 180 days after this Convention enters into force for the State Party or after the facility has been declared for the first time, except for a chemical weapons destruction facility to which paragraphs 5 to 7 shall apply.

5.   In the case of a chemical weapons destruction facility that begins operations more than one year after this Convention enters into force for the State Party, the facility agreement shall be completed not less than 180 days before the facility begins operation.

6.   In the case of a chemical weapons destruction facility that is in operation when this Convention enters into force for the State Party, or begins operation not later than one year thereafter, the facility agreement shall be completed not later than 210 days after this Convention enters into force for the State Party, except that the Executive Council may decide that transitional verification arrangements, approved in accordance with Part IV (A), paragraph 51, of this Annex and including a transitional facility agreement, provisions for verification through on-site inspection and monitoring with on-site instruments, and the time-frame for application of the arrangements, are sufficient.

7.   In the case of a facility, referred to in paragraph 6, that will cease operations not later than two years after this Convention enters into force for the

State Party, the Executive Council may decide that transitional verification arrangements, approved in accordance with Part IV (A), paragraph 51, of this Annex and including a transitional facility agreement, provisions for verification through on-site inspection and monitoring with on-site instruments, and the time-frame for application of the arrangements, are sufficient.

8. Facility agreements shall be based on models for such agreements and provide for detailed arrangements which shall govern inspections at each facility. The model agreements shall include provisions to take into account future technological developments and shall be considered and approved by the Conference pursuant to Article VIII, paragraph 21 (*i*).

9. The Technical Secretariat may retain at each site a sealed container for photographs, plans and other information that it may wish to refer to in the course of subsequent inspections.

B. STANDING ARRANGEMENTS

10. Where applicable, the Technical Secretariat shall have the right to have continuous monitoring instruments and systems and seals installed and to use them, in conformity with the relevant provisions in this Convention and the facility agreements between States Parties and the Organization.

11. The inspected State Party shall, in accordance with agreed procedures, have the right to inspect any instrument used or installed by the inspection team and to have it tested in the presence of representatives of the inspected State Party. The inspection team shall have the right to use the instruments that were installed by the inspected State Party for its own monitoring of the technological process of the destruction of chemical weapons. To this end, the inspection team shall have the right to inspect those instruments that it intends to use for purposes of verification of the destruction of chemical weapons and to have them tested in its presence.

12. The inspected State Party shall provide the necessary preparation and support for the establishment of continuous monitoring instruments and systems.

13. In order to implement paragraphs 11 and 12, appropriate detailed procedures shall be considered and approved by the Conference pursuant to Article VIII, paragraph 21 (*i*).

14. The inspected State Party shall immediately notify the Technical Secretariat if an event occurs or may occur at a facility where monitoring instruments are installed, which may have an impact on the monitoring system. The inspected State Party shall coordinate subsequent actions with the Technical Secretariat with

a view to restoring the operation of the monitoring system and establishing interim measures, if necessary, as soon as possible.

15. The inspection team shall verify during each inspection that the monitoring system functions correctly and that emplaced seals have not been tampered with. In addition, visits to service the monitoring system may be required to perform any necessary maintenance or replacement of equipment, or to adjust the coverage of the monitoring system as required.

16. If the monitoring system indicates any anomaly, the Technical Secretariat shall immediately take action to determine whether this resulted from equipment malfunction or activities at the facility. If, after this examination, the problem remains unresolved, the Technical Secretariat shall immediately ascertain the actual situation, including through immediate on-site inspection of, or visit to, the facility if necessary. The Technical Secretariat shall report any such problem immediately after its detection to the inspected State Party which shall assist in its resolution.

C. Pre-inspection activities

17. The inspected State Party shall, except as specified in paragraph 18, be notified of inspections not less than 24 hours in advance of the planned arrival of the inspection team at the point of entry.

18. The inspected State Party shall be notified of initial inspections not less than 72 hours in advance of the estimated time of arrival of the inspection team at the point of entry.

PART IV (A)

DESTRUCTION OF CHEMICAL WEAPONS AND ITS VERIFICATION
PURSUANT TO ARTICLE IV

A. DECLARATIONS

Chemical weapons

1.   The declaration of chemical weapons by a State Party pursuant to Article III, paragraph 1 (*a*) (ii), shall include the following:

(*a*) The aggregate quantity of each chemical declared;

(*b*) The precise location of each chemical weapons storage facility, expressed by:

    (i)   Name;

    (ii) Geographical coordinates; and

    (iii) A detailed site diagram, including a boundary map and the location of bunkers/storage areas within the facility.

(*c*) The detailed inventory for each chemical weapons storage facility including:

    (i)   Chemicals defined as chemical weapons in accordance with Article II;

    (ii) Unfilled munitions, sub-munitions, devices and equipment defined as chemical weapons;

    (iii) Equipment specially designed for use directly in connection with the employment of munitions, sub-munitions, devices or equipment specified in sub-subparagraph (ii);

    (iv) Chemicals specifically designed for use directly in connection with the employment of munitions, sub-munitions, devices or equipment specified in sub-subparagraph (ii).

2.   For the declaration of chemicals referred to in paragraph 1 (*c*) (i) the following shall apply:

(*a*) Chemicals shall be declared in accordance with the Schedules specified in the Annex on Chemicals;

(*b*)   For a chemical not listed in the Schedules in the Annex on Chemicals the information required for possible assignment of the chemical to the appropriate Schedule shall be provided, including the toxicity of the pure compound. For a precursor, the toxicity and identity of the principal final reaction product(s) shall be provided;

(*c*)   Chemicals shall be identified by chemical name in accordance with current International Union of Pure and Applied Chemistry (IUPAC) nomenclature, structural formula and Chemical Abstracts Service registry number, if assigned. For a precursor, the toxicity and identity of the principal final reaction product(s) shall be provided;

(*d*)   In cases involving mixtures of two or more chemicals, each chemical shall be identified and the percentage of each shall be provided, and the mixture shall be declared under the category of the most toxic chemical. If a component of a binary chemical weapon consists of a mixture of two or more chemicals, each chemical shall be identified and the percentage of each provided;

(*e*)   Binary chemical weapons shall be declared under the relevant end product within the framework of the categories of chemical weapons referred to in paragraph 16. The following supplementary information shall be provided for each type of binary chemical munition/device:

(i)   The chemical name of the toxic end-product;

(ii)   The chemical composition and quantity of each component;

(iii)   The actual weight ratio between the components;

(iv)   Which component is considered the key component;

(v)   The projected quantity of the toxic end-product calculated on a stoichiometric basis from the key component, assuming 100 per cent yield. A declared quantity (in tonnes) of the key component intended for a specific toxic end-product shall be considered equivalent to the quantity (in tonnes) of this toxic end-product calculated on a stoichiometric basis assuming 100 per cent yield.

(*f*)   For multicomponent chemical weapons, the declaration shall be analogous to that envisaged for binary chemical weapons;

(*g*)   For each chemical the form of storage, i.e. munitions, submunitions, devices, equipment or bulk containers and other containers shall be declared. For each form of storage the following shall be listed:

     (i)   Type;

    (ii)   Size or calibre;

  (iii)   Number of items; and

  (iv)   Nominal weight of chemical fill per item.

(*h*) For each chemical the total weight present at the storage facility shall be declared;

(*i*) In addition, for chemicals stored in bulk, the percentage purity shall be declared, if known.

3.   For each type of unfilled munitions, sub-munitions, devices or equipment, referred to in paragraph 1 (*c*) (ii), the information shall include:

(*a*) The number of items;

(*b*) The nominal fill volume per item;

(*c*) The intended chemical fill.

Declarations of chemical weapons pursuant to Article III, paragraph 1 (a) (iii)

4.   The declaration of chemical weapons pursuant to Article III, paragraph 1 (*a*) (iii), shall contain all information specified in paragraphs 1 to 3 above. It is the responsibility of the State Party on whose territory the chemical weapons are located to make appropriate arrangements with the other State to ensure that the declarations are made. If the State Party on whose territory the chemical weapons are located is not able to fulfil its obligations under this paragraph, it shall state the reasons therefor.

Declarations of past transfers and receipts

5.   A State Party that has transferred or received chemical weapons since 1 January 1946 shall declare these transfers or receipts pursuant to Article III, paragraph 1 (*a*) (iv), provided the amount transferred or received exceeded 1 tonne per chemical per year in bulk and/or munition form. This declaration shall be made according to the inventory format specified in paragraphs 1 and 2. This declaration shall also indicate the supplier and recipient countries, the dates of the transfers or receipts and, as precisely as possible, the current location of the transferred items. When not all the specified information is available for transfers or receipts of chemical weapons for the period between 1 January 1946 and 1 January 1970, the State Party shall declare whatever information is still available to it and provide an explanation as to why it cannot submit a full declaration.

Submission of the general plan for destruction of chemical weapons

6.   The general plan for destruction of chemical weapons submitted pursuant to Article III, paragraph 1 (*a*) (v), shall provide an overview of the entire national chemical weapons destruction programme of the State Party and information on the efforts of the State Party to fulfil the destruction requirements contained in this Convention. The plan shall specify:

(*a*)   A general schedule for destruction, giving types and approximate quantities of chemical weapons planned to be destroyed in each annual destruction period for each existing chemical weapons destruction facility and, if possible, for each planned chemical weapons destruction facility;

(*b*)   The number of chemical weapons destruction facilities existing or planned to be operated over the destruction period;

(*c*)   For each existing or planned chemical weapons destruction facility:

   (i)   Name and location; and

   (ii)   The types and approximate quantities of chemical weapons, and the type (for example, nerve agent or blister agent) and approximate quantity of chemical fill, to be destroyed;

(*d*)   The plans and programmes for training personnel for the operation of destruction facilities;

(*e*)   The national standards for safety and emissions that the destruction facilities must satisfy;

(*f*)   Information on the development of new methods for destruction of chemical weapons and on the improvement of existing methods;

(*g*)   The cost estimates for destroying the chemical weapons; and

(*h*)   Any issues which could adversely impact on the national destruction programme.

B.   MEASURES TO SECURE THE STORAGE FACILITY
AND STORAGE FACILITY PREPARATION

7.   Not later than when submitting its declaration of chemical weapons, a State Party shall take such measures as it considers appropriate to secure its storage facilities and shall prevent any movement of its chemical weapons out of the facilities, except their removal for destruction.

8.   A State Party shall ensure that chemical weapons at its storage facilities are configured to allow ready access for verification in accordance with paragraphs 37 to 49.

9.   While a storage facility remains closed for any movement of chemical weapons out of the facility other than their removal for destruction, a State Party may continue at the facility standard maintenance activities, including standard maintenance of chemical weapons; safety monitoring and physical security activities; and preparation of chemical weapons for destruction.

10.   Maintenance activities of chemical weapons shall not include:

(*a*)   Replacement of agent or of munition bodies;

(*b*)   Modification of the original characteristics of munitions, or parts or components thereof.

11.   All maintenance activities shall be subject to monitoring by the Technical Secretariat.

C.   DESTRUCTION

Principles and methods for destruction of chemical weapons

12.   "Destruction of chemical weapons" means a process by which chemicals are converted in an essentially irreversible way to a form unsuitable for production of chemical weapons, and which in an irreversible manner renders munitions and other devices unusable as such.

13.   Each State Party shall determine how it shall destroy chemical weapons, except that the following processes may not be used: dumping in any body of water, land burial or open-pit burning. It shall destroy chemical weapons only at specifically designated and appropriately designed and equipped facilities.

14.   Each State Party shall ensure that its chemical weapons destruction facilities are constructed and operated in a manner to ensure the destruction of the chemical weapons; and that the destruction process can be verified under the provisions of this Convention.

Order of destruction

15.   The order of destruction of chemical weapons is based on the obligations specified in Article I and the other Articles, including obligations regarding systematic on-site verification. It takes into account interests of States Parties for undiminished security during the destruction period; confidence-building in the early part of the destruction stage; gradual acquisition of experience in the course of destroying chemical weapons; and applicability irrespective of the actual composition

of the stockpiles and the methods chosen for the destruction of the chemical weapons. The order of destruction is based on the principle of levelling out.

16. For the purpose of destruction, chemical weapons declared by each State Party shall be divided into three categories:

Category 1: Chemical weapons on the basis of Schedule 1 chemicals and their parts and components;

Category 2: Chemical weapons on the basis of all other chemicals and their parts and components;

Category 3: Unfilled munitions and devices, and equipment specifically designed for use directly in connection with employment of chemical weapons.

17. A State Party shall start:

(a) The destruction of Category 1 chemical weapons not later than two years after this Convention enters into force for it, and shall complete the destruction not later than 10 years after entry into force of this Convention. A State Party shall destroy chemical weapons in accordance with the following destruction deadlines:

(i) Phase 1: Not later than two years after entry into force of this Convention, testing of its first destruction facility shall be completed. Not less than 1 per cent of the Category 1 chemical weapons shall be destroyed not later than three years after the entry into force of this Convention;

(ii) Phase 2: Not less than 20 per cent of the Category 1 chemical weapons shall be destroyed not later than five years after the entry into force of this Convention;

(iii) Phase 3: Not less than 45 per cent of the Category 1 chemical weapons shall be destroyed not later than seven years after the entry into force of this Convention;

(iv) Phase 4: All Category 1 chemical weapons shall be destroyed not later than 10 years after the entry into force of this Convention.

(b) The destruction of Category 2 chemical weapons not later than one year after this Convention enters into force for it and shall complete the destruction not later than five years after the entry into force of this Convention. Category 2 chemical weapons shall be destroyed in equal annual increments throughout the destruction period. The comparison factor for such weapons is the weight of the chemicals within Category 2; and

(c) The destruction of Category 3 chemical weapons not later than one year after this Convention enters into force for it, and shall complete the destruction not later than five years after the entry into force of this Convention. Category 3 chemical weapons shall be destroyed in equal annual increments throughout the destruction period. The comparison factor for unfilled munitions and devices is expressed in nominal fill volume (m^3) and for equipment in number of items.

18. For the destruction of binary chemical weapons the following shall apply:

(a) For the purposes of the order of destruction, a declared quantity (in tonnes) of the key component intended for a specific toxic end-product shall be considered equivalent to the quantity (in tonnes) of this toxic end-product calculated on a stoichiometric basis assuming 100 per cent yield.

(b) A requirement to destroy a given quantity of the key component shall entail a requirement to destroy a corresponding quantity of the other component, calculated from the actual weight ratio of the components in the relevant type of binary chemical munition/device.

(c) If more of the other component is declared than is needed, based on the actual weight ratio between components, the excess shall be destroyed over the first two years after destruction operations begin.

(d) At the end of each subsequent operational year a State Party may retain an amount of the other declared component that is determined on the basis of the actual weight ratio of the components in the relevant type of binary chemical munition/device.

19. For multicomponent chemical weapons the order of destruction shall be analogous to that envisaged for binary chemical weapons.

Modification of intermediate destruction deadlines

20. The Executive Council shall review the general plans for destruction of chemical weapons, submitted pursuant to Article III, paragraph 1 (a) (v), and in accordance with paragraph 6, *inter alia*, to assess their conformity with the order of destruction set forth in paragraphs 15 to 19. The Executive Council shall consult with any State Party whose plan does not conform, with the objective of bringing the plan into conformity.

21. If a State Party, due to exceptional circumstances beyond its control, believes that it cannot achieve the level of destruction specified for Phase 1, Phase 2 or Phase 3 of the order of destruction of Category 1 chemical weapons, it may propose changes in those levels. Such a proposal must be made not later than 120 days after the entry into force of this Convention and shall contain a detailed explanation of the reasons for the proposal.

22. Each State Party shall take all necessary measures to ensure destruction of Category 1 chemical weapons in accordance with the destruction deadlines set forth in paragraph 17 (*a*) as changed pursuant to paragraph 21. However, if a State Party believes that it will be unable to ensure the destruction of the percentage of Category 1 chemical weapons required by an intermediate destruction deadline, it may request the Executive Council to recommend to the Conference to grant an extension of its obligation to meet that deadline. Such a request must be made not less than 180 days before the intermediate destruction deadline and shall contain a detailed explanation of the reasons for the request and the plans of the State Party for ensuring that it will be able to fulfil its obligation to meet the next intermediate destruction deadline.

23. If an extension is granted, the State Party shall still be under the obligation to meet the cumulative destruction requirements set forth for the next destruction deadline. Extensions granted pursuant to this Section shall not, in any way, modify the obligation of the State Party to destroy all Category 1 chemical weapons not later than 10 years after the entry into force of this Convention.

Extension of the deadline for completion of destruction

24. If a State Party believes that it will be unable to ensure the destruction of all Category 1 chemical weapons not later than 10 years after the entry into force of this Convention, it may submit a request to the Executive Council for an extension of the deadline for completing the destruction of such chemical weapons. Such a request must be made not later than nine years after the entry into force of this Convention.

25. The request shall contain:

(*a*)   The duration of the proposed extension;

(*b*)   A detailed explanation of the reasons for the proposed extension; and

(*c*)   A detailed plan for destruction during the proposed extension and the remaining portion of the original 10-year period for destruction.

26. A decision on the request shall be taken by the Conference at its next session, on the recommendation of the Executive Council. Any extension shall be the minimum necessary, but in no case shall the deadline for a State Party to complete its destruction of all chemical weapons be extended beyond 15 years after the entry into force of this Convention. The Executive Council shall set conditions for the granting of the extension, including the specific verification measures deemed necessary as well as specific actions to be taken by the State Party to overcome problems in its destruction programme. Costs of verification during the extension period shall be allocated in accordance with Article IV, paragraph 16.

27. If an extension is granted, the State Party shall take appropriate measures to meet all subsequent deadlines.

28. The State Party shall continue to submit detailed annual plans for destruction in accordance with paragraph 29 and annual reports on the destruction of Category 1 chemical weapons in accordance with paragraph 36, until all Category 1 chemical weapons are destroyed. In addition, not later than at the end of each 90 days of the extension period, the State Party shall report to the Executive Council on its destruction activity. The Executive Council shall review progress towards completion of destruction and take the necessary measures to document this progress. All information concerning the destruction activities during the extension period shall be provided by the Executive Council to States Parties, upon request.

Detailed annual plans for destruction

29. The detailed annual plans for destruction shall be submitted to the Technical Secretariat not less than 60 days before each annual destruction period begins pursuant to Article IV, paragraph 7 (*a*), and shall specify:

(*a*) The quantity of each specific type of chemical weapon to be destroyed at each destruction facility and the inclusive dates when the destruction of each specific type of chemical weapon will be accomplished;

(*b*) The detailed site diagram for each chemical weapons destruction facility and any changes to previously submitted diagrams; and

(*c*) The detailed schedule of activities for each chemical weapons destruction facility for the upcoming year, identifying time required for design, construction or modification of the facility, installation of equipment, equipment check-out and operator training, destruction operations for each specific type of chemical weapon, and scheduled periods of inactivity.

30. A State Party shall provide, for each of its chemical weapons destruction facilities, detailed facility information to assist the Technical Secretariat in developing preliminary inspection procedures for use at the facility.

31. The detailed facility information for each destruction facility shall include the following information:

(*a*) Name, address and location;

(*b*) Detailed, annotated facility drawings;

(c) Facility design drawings, process drawings, and piping and instrumentation design drawings;

(d) Detailed technical descriptions, including design drawings and instrument specifications, for the equipment required for: removing the chemical fill from the munitions, devices, and containers; temporarily storing the drained chemical fill; destroying the chemical agent; and destroying the munitions, devices, and containers;

(e) Detailed technical descriptions of the destruction process, including material flow rates, temperatures and pressures, and designed destruction efficiency;

(f) Design capacity for each specific type of chemical weapon;

(g) A detailed description of the products of destruction and the method of their ultimate disposal;

(h) A detailed technical description of measures to facilitate inspections in accordance with this Convention;

(i) A detailed description of any temporary holding area at the destruction facility that will be used to provide chemical weapons directly to the destruction facility, including site and facility drawings and information on the storage capacity for each specific type of chemical weapon to be destroyed at the facility;

(j) A detailed description of the safety and medical measures in force at the facility;

(k) A detailed description of the living quarters and working premises for the inspectors; and

(l) Suggested measures for international verification.

32. A State Party shall provide, for each of its chemical weapons destruction facilities, the plant operations manuals, the safety and medical plans, the laboratory operations and quality assurance and control manuals, and the environmental permits that have been obtained, except that this shall not include material previously provided.

33. A State Party shall promptly notify the Technical Secretariat of any developments that could affect inspection activities at its destruction facilities.

34. Deadlines for submission of the information specified in paragraphs 30 to 32 shall be considered and approved by the Conference pursuant to Article VIII, paragraph 21 (i).

35. After a review of the detailed facility information for each destruction facility, the Technical Secretariat, if the need arises, shall enter into consultation with the State Party concerned in order to ensure that its chemical weapons destruction facilities are designed to assure the destruction of chemical weapons, to allow advanced planning on how verification measures may be applied and to ensure that the application of verification measures is consistent with proper facility operation, and that the facility operation allows appropriate verification.

Annual reports on destruction

36. Information regarding the implementation of plans for destruction of chemical weapons shall be submitted to the Technical Secretariat pursuant to Article IV, paragraph 7 (*b*), not later than 60 days after the end of each annual destruction period and shall specify the actual amounts of chemical weapons which were destroyed during the previous year at each destruction facility. If appropriate, reasons for not meeting destruction goals should be stated.

D. VERIFICATION

Verification of declarations of chemical weapons through on-site inspection

37. The purpose of the verification of declarations of chemical weapons shall be to confirm through on-site inspection the accuracy of the relevant declarations made pursuant to Article III.

38. The inspectors shall conduct this verification promptly after a declaration is submitted. They shall, *inter alia,* verify the quantity and identity of chemicals, types and number of munitions, devices and other equipment.

39. The inspectors shall employ, as appropriate, agreed seals, markers or other inventory control procedures to facilitate an accurate inventory of the chemical weapons at each storage facility.

40. As the inventory progresses, inspectors shall install such agreed seals as may be necessary to clearly indicate if any stocks are removed, and to ensure the securing of the storage facility during the inventory. After completion of the inventory, such seals will be removed unless otherwise agreed.

Systematic verification of storage facilities

41. The purpose of the systematic verification of storage facilities shall be to ensure that no undetected removal of chemical weapons from such facilities takes place.

42. The systematic verification shall be initiated as soon as possible after the declaration of chemical weapons is submitted and shall continue until all chemical weapons have been removed from the storage facility. It shall in accordance with the facility agreement, combine on-site inspection and monitoring with on-site instruments.

43. When all chemical weapons have been removed from the storage facility, the Technical Secretariat shall confirm the declaration of the State Party to that effect. After this confirmation, the Technical Secretariat shall terminate the systematic verification of the storage facility and shall promptly remove any monitoring instruments installed by the inspectors.

Inspections and visits

44. The particular storage facility to be inspected shall be chosen by the Technical Secretariat in such a way as to preclude the prediction of precisely when the facility is to be inspected. The guidelines for determining the frequency of systematic on-site inspections shall be elaborated by the Technical Secretariat, taking into account the recommendations to be considered and approved by the Conference pursuant to Article VIII, paragraph 21 (*i*).

45. The Technical Secretariat shall notify the inspected State Party of its decision to inspect or visit the storage facility 48 hours before the planned arrival of the inspection team at the facility for systematic inspections or visits. In cases of inspections or visits to resolve urgent problems, this period may be shortened. The Technical Secretariat shall specify the purpose of the inspection or visit.

46. The inspected State Party shall make any necessary preparations for the arrival of the inspectors and shall ensure their expeditious transportation from their point of entry to the storage facility. The facility agreement will specify administrative arrangements for inspectors.

47. The inspected State Party shall provide the inspection team upon its arrival at the chemical weapons storage facility to carry out an inspection, with the following data on the facility:

(*a*)   The number of storage buildings and storage locations;

(*b*)   For each storage building and storage location, the type and the identification number or designation, shown on the site diagram; and

(*c*)   For each storage building and storage location at the facility, the number of items of each specific type of chemical weapon, and, for containers that are not part of binary munitions, the actual quantity of chemical fill in each container.

48. In carrying out an inventory, within the time available, inspectors shall have the right:

(a) To use any of the following inspection techniques:

  (i) inventory all the chemical weapons stored at the facility;

  (ii) inventory all the chemical weapons stored in specific buildings or locations at the facility, as chosen by the inspectors; or

  (iii) inventory all the chemical weapons of one or more specific types stored at the facility, as chosen by the inspectors; and

(b) To check all items inventoried against agreed records.

49. Inspectors shall, in accordance with facility agreements:

(a) Have unimpeded access to all parts of the storage facilities including any munitions, devices, bulk containers, or other containers therein. While conducting their activity, inspectors shall comply with the safety regulations at the facility. The items to be inspected will be chosen by the inspectors; and

(b) Have the right, during the first and any subsequent inspection of each chemical weapons storage facility, to designate munitions, devices, and containers from which samples are to be taken, and to affix to such munitions, devices, and containers a unique tag that will indicate an attempt to remove or alter the tag. A sample shall be taken from a tagged item at a chemical weapons storage facility or a chemical weapons destruction facility as soon as it is practically possible in accordance with the corresponding destruction programmes, and, in any case, not later than by the end of the destruction operations.

Systematic verification of the destruction of chemical weapons

50. The purpose of verification of destruction of chemical weapons shall be:

(a) To confirm the identity and quantity of the chemical weapons stocks to be destroyed; and

(b) To confirm that these stocks have been destroyed.

51. Chemical weapons destruction operations during the first 390 days after the entry into force of this Convention shall be governed by transitional verification arrangements. Such arrangements, including a transitional facility agreement, provisions for verification through on-site inspection and monitoring with on-site instruments, and the time-frame for application of the arrangements, shall be agreed

between the Organization and the inspected State Party. These arrangements shall be approved by the Executive Council not later than 60 days after this Convention enters into force for the State Party, taking into account the recommendations of the Technical Secretariat, which shall be based on an evaluation of the detailed facility information provided in accordance with paragraph 31 and a visit to the facility. The Executive Council shall, at its first session, establish the guidelines for such transitional verification arrangements, based on recommendations to be considered and approved by the Conference pursuant to Article VIII, paragraph 21 (*i*). The transitional verification arrangements shall be designed to verify, throughout the entire transitional period, the destruction of chemical weapons in accordance with the purposes set forth in paragraph 50, and to avoid hampering ongoing destruction operations.

52. The provisions of paragraphs 53 to 61 shall apply to chemical weapons destruction operations that are to begin not earlier than 390 days after the entry into force of this Convention.

53. On the basis of this Convention and the detailed destruction facility information, and as the case may be, on experience from previous inspections, the Technical Secretariat shall prepare a draft plan for inspecting the destruction of chemical weapons at each destruction facility. The plan shall be completed and provided to the inspected State Party for comment not less than 270 days before the facility begins destruction operations pursuant to this Convention. Any differences between the Technical Secretariat and the inspected State Party should be resolved through consultations. Any unresolved matter shall be forwarded to the Executive Council for appropriate action with a view to facilitating the full implementation of this Convention.

54. The Technical Secretariat shall conduct an initial visit to each chemical weapons destruction facility of the inspected State Party not less than 240 days before each facility begins destruction operations pursuant to this Convention, to allow it to familiarize itself with the facility and assess the adequacy of the inspection plan.

55. In the case of an existing facility where chemical weapons destruction operations have already been initiated, the inspected State Party shall not be required to decontaminate the facility before the Technical Secretariat conducts an initial visit. The duration of the visit shall not exceed five days and the number of visiting personnel shall not exceed 15.

56. The agreed detailed plans for verification, with an appropriate recommendation by the Technical Secretariat, shall be forwarded to the Executive Council for review. The Executive Council shall review the plans with a view to approving them, consistent with verification objectives and obligations under this

Convention. It should also confirm that verification schemes for destruction are consistent with verification aims and are efficient and practical. This review should be completed not less than 180 days before the destruction period begins.

57. Each member of the Executive Council may consult with the Technical Secretariat on any issues regarding the adequacy of the plan for verification. If there are no objections by any member of the Executive Council, the plan shall be put into action.

58. If there are any difficulties, the Executive Council shall enter into consultations with the State Party to reconcile them. If any difficulties remain unresolved they shall be referred to the Conference.

59. The detailed facility agreements for chemical weapons destruction facilities shall specify, taking into account the specific characteristics of the destruction facility and its mode of operation:

(a)   Detailed on-site inspection procedures; and

(b)   Provisions for verification through continuous monitoring with on-site instruments and physical presence of inspectors.

60. Inspectors shall be granted access to each chemical weapons destruction facility not less than 60 days before the commencement of the destruction, pursuant to this Convention, at the facility. Such access shall be for the purpose of supervising the installation of the inspection equipment, inspecting this equipment and testing its operation, as well as for the purpose of carrying out a final engineering review of the facility. In the case of an existing facility where chemical weapons destruction operations have already been initiated, destruction operations shall be stopped for the minimum amount of time required, not to exceed 60 days, for installation and testing of the inspection equipment. Depending on the results of the testing and review, the State Party and the Technical Secretariat may agree on additions or changes to the detailed facility agreement for the facility.

61. The inspected State Party shall notify, in writing, the inspection team leader at a chemical weapons destruction facility not less than four hours before the departure of each shipment of chemical weapons from a chemical weapons storage facility to that destruction facility. This notification shall specify the name of the storage facility, the estimated times of departure and arrival, the specific types and quantities of chemical weapons being transported, whether any tagged items are being moved, and the method of transportation. This notification may include notification of more than one shipment. The inspection team leader shall be promptly notified, in writing, of any changes in this information.

*Chemical weapons storage facilities at chemical weapons
destruction facilities*

62. The inspectors shall verify the arrival of the chemical weapons at the destruction facility and the storing of these chemical weapons. The inspectors shall verify the inventory of each shipment, using agreed procedures consistent with facility safety regulations, prior to the destruction of the chemical weapons. They shall employ, as appropriate, agreed seals, markers or other inventory control procedures to facilitate an accurate inventory of the chemical weapons prior to destruction.

63. As soon and as long as chemical weapons are stored at chemical weapons storage facilities located at chemical weapons destruction facilities, these storage facilities shall be subject to systematic verification in conformity with the relevant facility agreements.

64. At the end of an active destruction phase, inspectors shall make an inventory of the chemical weapons, that have been removed from the storage facility, to be destroyed. They shall verify the accuracy of the inventory of the chemical weapons remaining, employing inventory control procedures as referred to in paragraph 62.

*Systematic on-site verification measures at chemical weapons
destruction facilities*

65. The inspectors shall be granted access to conduct their activities at the chemical weapons destruction facilities and the chemical weapons storage facilities located at such facilities during the entire active phase of destruction.

66. At each chemical weapons destruction facility, to provide assurance that no chemical weapons are diverted and that the destruction process has been completed, inspectors shall have the right to verify through their physical presence and monitoring with on-site instruments:

(*a*)   The receipt of chemical weapons at the facility;

(*b*)   The temporary holding area for chemical weapons and the specific type and quantity of chemical weapons stored in that area;

(*c*)   The specific type and quantity of chemical weapons being destroyed;

(*d*)   The process of destruction;

(*e*)   The end-product of destruction;

(*f*)   The mutilation of metal parts; and

(*g*)   The integrity of the destruction process and of the facility as a whole.

67.   Inspectors shall have the right to tag, for sampling, munitions, devices, or containers located in the temporary holding areas at the chemical weapons destruction facilities.

68.   To the extent that it meets inspection requirements, information from routine facility operations, with appropriate data authentication, shall be used for inspection purposes.

69.   After the completion of each period of destruction, the Technical Secretariat shall confirm the declaration of the State Party, reporting the completion of destruction of the designated quantity of chemical weapons.

70.   Inspectors shall, in accordance with facility agreements:

(*a*)   Have unimpeded access to all parts of the chemical weapons destruction facilities and the chemical weapons storage facilities located at such facilities, including any munitions, devices, bulk containers, or other containers, therein. The items to be inspected shall be chosen by the inspectors in accordance with the verification plan that has been agreed to by the inspected State Party and approved by the Executive Council;

(*b*)   Monitor the systematic on-site analysis of samples during the destruction process; and

(*c*)   Receive, if necessary, samples taken at their request from any devices, bulk containers and other containers at the destruction facility or the storage facility thereat.

Part IV (B)

Old chemical weapons and abandoned chemical weapons

A. General

1.   Old chemical weapons shall be destroyed as provided for in Section B.

2.   Abandoned chemical weapons, including those which also meet the definition of Article II, paragraph 5 (*b*), shall be destroyed as provided for in Section C.

B. Regime for old chemical weapons

3.   A State Party which has on its territory old chemical weapons as defined in Article II, paragraph 5 (*a*), shall, not later than 30 days after this Convention enters into force for it, submit to the Technical Secretariat all available relevant information, including, to the extent possible, the location, type, quantity and the present condition of these old chemical weapons.

In the case of old chemical weapons as defined in Article II, paragraph 5 (*b*), the State Party shall submit to the Technical Secretariat a declaration pursuant to Article III, paragraph 1 (*b*) (i), including, to the extent possible, the information specified in Part IV (A), paragraphs 1 to 3, of this Annex.

4.   A State Party which discovers old chemical weapons after this Convention enters into force for it shall submit to the Technical Secretariat the information specified in paragraph 3 not later than 180 days after the discovery of the old chemical weapons.

5.   The Technical Secretariat shall conduct an initial inspection, and any further inspections as may be necessary, in order to verify the information submitted pursuant to paragraphs 3 and 4 and in particular to determine whether the chemical weapons meet the definition of old chemical weapons as specified in Article II, paragraph 5. Guidelines to determine the usability of chemical weapons produced between 1925 and 1946 shall be considered and approved by the Conference pursuant to Article VIII, paragraph 21 (*i*).

6.   A State Party shall treat old chemical weapons that have been confirmed by the Technical Secretariat as meeting the definition in Article II, paragraph 5 (*a*), as toxic waste. It shall inform the Technical Secretariat of the steps being taken to destroy or otherwise dispose of such old chemical weapons as toxic waste in accordance with its national legislation.

7. Subject to paragraphs 3 to 5, a State Party shall destroy old chemical weapons that have been confirmed by the Technical Secretariat as meeting the definition in Article II, paragraph 5 (*b*), in accordance with Article IV and Part IV (A) of this Annex. Upon request of a State Party, the Executive Council may, however, modify the provisions on time-limit and order of destruction of these old chemical weapons, if it determines that doing so would not pose a risk to the object and purpose of this Convention. The request shall contain specific proposals for modification of the provisions and a detailed explanation of the reasons for the proposed modification.

C.   REGIME FOR ABANDONED CHEMICAL WEAPONS

8. A State Party on whose territory there are abandoned chemical weapons (hereinafter referred to as the "Territorial State Party") shall, not later than 30 days after this Convention enters into force for it, submit to the Technical Secretariat all available relevant information concerning the abandoned chemical weapons. This information shall include, to the extent possible, the location, type, quantity and the present condition of the abandoned chemical weapons as well as information on the abandonment.

9. A State Party which discovers abandoned chemical weapons after this Convention enters into force for it shall, not later than 180 days after the discovery, submit to the Technical Secretariat all available relevant information concerning the discovered abandoned chemical weapons. This information shall include, to the extent possible, the location, type, quantity and the present condition of the abandoned chemical weapons as well as information on the abandonment.

10. A State Party which has abandoned chemical weapons on the territory of another State Party (hereinafter referred to as the "Abandoning State Party") shall, not later than 30 days after this Convention enters into force for it, submit to the Technical Secretariat all available relevant information concerning the abandoned chemical weapons. This information shall include, to the extent possible, the location, type, quantity as well as information on the abandonment, and the condition of the abandoned chemical weapons.

11. The Technical Secretariat shall conduct an initial inspection, and any further inspections as may be necessary, in order to verify all available relevant information submitted pursuant to paragraphs 8 to 10 and determine whether systematic verification in accordance with Part IV (A), paragraphs 41 to 43, of this Annex is required. It shall, if necessary, verify the origin of the abandoned chemical weapons and establish evidence concerning the abandonment and the identity of the Abandoning State.

12. The report of the Technical Secretariat shall be submitted to the Executive Council, the Territorial State Party, and to the Abandoning State Party or the State Party declared by the Territorial State Party or identified by the Technical Secretariat as having abandoned the chemical weapons. If one of the States Parties directly concerned is not satisfied with the report it shall have the right to settle the matter in accordance with provisions of this Convention or bring the issue to the Executive Council with a view to settling the matter expeditiously.

13. Pursuant to Article I, paragraph 3, the Territorial State Party shall have the right to request the State Party which has been established as the Abandoning State Party pursuant to paragraphs 8 to 12 to enter into consultations for the purpose of destroying the abandoned chemical weapons in cooperation with the Territorial State Party. It shall immediately inform the Technical Secretariat of this request.

14. Consultations between the Territorial State Party and the Abandoning State Party with a view to establishing a mutually agreed plan for destruction shall begin not later than 30 days after the Technical Secretariat has been informed of the request referred to in paragraph 13. The mutually agreed plan for destruction shall be transmitted to the Technical Secretariat not later than 180 days after the Technical Secretariat has been informed of the request referred to in paragraph 13. Upon the request of the Abandoning State Party and the Territorial State Party, the Executive Council may extend the time-limit for transmission of the mutually agreed plan for destruction.

15. For the purpose of destroying abandoned chemical weapons, the Abandoning State Party shall provide all necessary financial, technical, expert, facility as well as other resources. The Territorial State Party shall provide appropriate cooperation.

16. If the Abandoning State cannot be identified or is not a State Party, the Territorial State Party, in order to ensure the destruction of these abandoned chemical weapons, may request the Organization and other States Parties to provide assistance in the destruction of these abandoned chemical weapons.

17. Subject to paragraphs 8 to 16, Article IV and Part IV (A) of this Annex shall also apply to the destruction of abandoned chemical weapons. In the case of abandoned chemical weapons which also meet the definition of old chemical weapons in Article II, paragraph 5 (*b*), the Executive Council, upon the request of the Territorial State Party, individually or together with the Abandoning State Party, may modify or in exceptional cases suspend the application of provisions on destruction, if it determines that doing so would not pose a risk to the object and purpose of this Convention. In the case of abandoned chemical weapons which do not meet the definition of old chemical weapons in Article II, paragraph 5 (*b*), the Executive Council, upon the request of the Territorial State Party, individually or

together with the Abandoning State Party, may in exceptional circumstances modify the provisions on the time-limit and the order of destruction, if it determines that doing so would not pose a risk to the object and purpose of this Convention. Any request as referred to in this paragraph shall contain specific proposals for modification of the provisions and a detailed explanation of the reasons for the proposed modification.

18. States Parties may conclude between themselves agreements or arrangements concerning the destruction of abandoned chemical weapons. The Executive Council may, upon request of the Territorial State Party, individually or together with the Abandoning State Party, decide that selected provisions of such agreements or arrangements take precedence over provisions of this Section, if it determines that the agreement or arrangement ensures the destruction of the abandoned chemical weapons in accordance with paragraph 17.

PART V

DESTRUCTION OF CHEMICAL WEAPONS PRODUCTION FACILITIES AND ITS
VERIFICATION PURSUANT TO ARTICLE V

A. DECLARATIONS

Declarations of chemical weapons production facilities

1.   The declaration of chemical weapons production facilities by a State Party pursuant to Article III, paragraph 1 (*c*) (ii), shall contain for each facility:

(*a*)   The name of the facility, the names of the owners, and the names of the companies or enterprises operating the facility since 1 January 1946;

(*b*)   The precise location of the facility, including the address, location of the complex, location of the facility within the complex including the specific building and structure number, if any;

(*c*)   A statement whether it is a facility for the manufacture of chemicals that are defined as chemical weapons or whether it is a facility for the filling of chemical weapons, or both;

(*d*) The date when the construction of the facility was completed and the periods during which any modifications to the facility were made, including the installation of new or modified equipment, that significantly changed the production process characteristics of the facility;

(*e*) Information on the chemicals defined as chemical weapons that were manufactured at the facility; the munitions, devices, and containers that were filled at the facility; and the dates of the beginning and cessation of such manufacture or filling:

(i)   For chemicals defined as chemical weapons that were manufactured at the facility, such information shall be expressed in terms of the specific types of chemicals manufactured, indicating the chemical name in accordance with the current International Union of Pure and Applied Chemistry (IUPAC) nomenclature, structural formula, and the Chemical Abstracts Service registry number, if assigned, and in terms of the amount of each chemical expressed by weight of chemical in tonnes;

(ii)   For munitions, devices and containers that were filled at the facility, such information shall be expressed in terms of the specific type of chemical weapons filled and the weight of the chemical fill per unit;

(*f*)   The production capacity of the chemical weapons production facility:

  (i)   For a facility where chemical weapons were manufactured, production capacity shall be expressed in terms of the annual quantitative potential for manufacturing a specific substance on the basis of the technological process actually used or, in the case of processes not actually used, planned to be used at the facility;

  (ii)   For a facility where chemical weapons were filled, production capacity shall be expressed in terms of the quantity of chemical that the facility can fill into each specific type of chemical weapon a year;

(*g*)   For each chemical weapons production facility that has not been destroyed, a description of the facility including:

  (i)   A site diagram;

  (ii)   A process flow diagram of the facility; and

  (iii)   An inventory of buildings at the facility, and specialized equipment at the facility and of any spare parts for such equipment;

(*h*)   The present status of the facility, stating:

  (i)   The date when chemical weapons were last produced at the facility;

  (ii)   Whether the facility has been destroyed, including the date and manner of its destruction; and

  (iii)   Whether the facility has been used or modified before entry into force of this Convention for an activity not related to the production of chemical weapons, and if so, information on what modifications have been made, the date such non-chemical weapons related activity began and the nature of such activity, indicating, if applicable, the kind of product;

(*i*)   A specification of the measures that have been taken by the State Party for closure of, and a description of the measures that have been or will be taken by the State Party to inactivate the facility;

(*j*)   A description of the normal pattern of activity for safety and security at the inactivated facility; and (*k*) A statement as to whether the facility will be converted for the destruction of chemical weapons and, if so, the dates for such conversions.

Declarations of chemical weapons production facilities pursuant to Article III, paragraph 1 (c) (iii)

2. The declaration of chemical weapons production facilities pursuant to Article III, paragraph 1 (*c*) (iii), shall contain all information specified in paragraph 1 above. It is the responsibility of the State Party on whose territory the facility is or has been located to make appropriate arrangements with the other State to ensure that the declarations are made. If the State Party on whose territory the facility is or has been located is not able to fulfil this obligation, it shall state the reasons therefor.

Declarations of past transfers and receipts

3. A State Party that has transferred or received chemical weapons production equipment since 1 January 1946 shall declare these transfers and receipts pursuant to Article III, paragraph 1 (*c*) (iv), and in accordance with paragraph 5 below. When not all the specified information is available for transfer and receipt of such equipment for the period between 1 January 1946 and 1 January 1970, the State Party shall declare whatever information is still available to it and provide an explanation as to why it cannot submit a full declaration.

4. Chemical weapons production equipment referred to in paragraph 3 means:

(*a*) Specialized equipment;

(*b*) Equipment for the production of equipment specifically designed for use directly in connection with chemical weapons employment; and

(*c*) Equipment designed or used exclusively for producing non-chemical parts for chemical munitions.

5. The declaration concerning transfer and receipt of chemical weapons production equipment shall specify:

(*a*) Who received/transferred the chemical weapons production equipment;

(*b*) The identity of such equipment;

(*c*) The date of transfer or receipt;

(*d*) Whether the equipment was destroyed, if known; and

(*e*)   Current disposition, if known.

Submission of general plans for destruction

6.   For each chemical weapons production facility, a State Party shall supply the following information:

(*a*)   Envisaged time-frame for measures to be taken; and

(*b*)   Methods of destruction.

7.   For each chemical weapons production facility that a State Party intends to convert temporarily into a chemical weapons destruction facility, the State Party shall supply the following information:

(*a*)   Envisaged time-frame for conversion into a destruction facility;

(*b*)   Envisaged time-frame for utilizing the facility as a chemical weapons destruction facility;

(*c*)   Description of the new facility;

(*d*)   Method of destruction of special equipment;

(*e*)   Time-frame for destruction of the converted facility after it has been utilized to destroy chemical weapons; and

(*f*)   Method of destruction of the converted facility.

Submission of annual plans for destruction and
annual reports on destruction

8.   The State Party shall submit an annual plan for destruction not less than 90 days before the beginning of the coming destruction year. The annual plan shall specify:

(*a*)   Capacity to be destroyed;

(*b*)   Name and location of the facilities where destruction will take place;

(*c*)   List of buildings and equipment that will be destroyed at each facility; and

(*d*)   Planned method(s) of destruction.

9.   A State Party shall submit an annual report on destruction not later than 90 days after the end of the previous destruction year. The annual report shall specify:

(a) Capacity destroyed;

(b) Name and location of each facility where destruction took place;

(c) List of buildings and equipment that were destroyed at each facility;

(d) Methods of destruction.

10. For a chemical weapons production facility declared pursuant to Article III, paragraph 1 *(c)* (iii), it is the responsibility of the State Party on whose territory the facility is or has been located to make appropriate arrangements to ensure that the declarations specified in paragraphs 6 to 9 above are made. If the State Party on whose territory the facility is or has been located is not able to fulfil this obligation, it shall state the reasons therefor.

B. DESTRUCTION

General principles for destruction of chemical weapons production facilities

11. Each State Party shall decide on methods to be applied for the destruction of chemical weapons production facilities, according to the principles laid down in Article V and in this Part.

Principles and methods for closure of a chemical weapons production facility

12. The purpose of the closure of a chemical weapons production facility is to render it inactive.

13. Agreed measures for closure shall be taken by a State Party with due regard to the specific characteristics of each facility. Such measures shall include, *inter alia*:

(a) Prohibition of occupation of the specialized buildings and standard buildings of the facility except for agreed activities;

(b) Disconnection of equipment directly related to the production of chemical weapons, including, *inter alia,* process control equipment and utilities;

(c) Decommissioning of protective installations and equipment used exclusively for the safety of operations of the chemical weapons production facility;

(*d*)   Installation of blind flanges and other devices to prevent the addition of chemicals to, or the removal of chemicals from, any specialized process equipment for synthesis, separation or purification of chemicals defined as a chemical weapon, any storage tank, or any machine for filling chemical weapons, the heating, cooling, or supply of electrical or other forms of power to such equipment, storage tanks, or machines; and

(*e*)   Interruption of rail, road and other access routes for heavy transport to the chemical weapons production facility except those required for agreed activities.

14.   While the chemical weapons production facility remains closed, a State Party may continue safety and physical security activities at the facility.

Technical maintenance of chemical weapons production facilities prior to their destruction

15.   A State Party may carry out standard maintenance activities at chemical weapons production facilities only for safety reasons, including visual inspection, preventive maintenance, and routine repairs.

16.   All planned maintenance activities shall be specified in the general and detailed plans for destruction. Maintenance activities shall not include:

(*a*)   Replacement of any process equipment;

(*b*)   Modification of the characteristics of the chemical process equipment;

(*c*)   Production of chemicals of any type.

17.   All maintenance activities shall be subject to monitoring by the Technical Secretariat.

Principles and methods for temporary conversion of chemical weapons production facilities into chemical weapons destruction facilities

18.   Measures pertaining to the temporary conversion of chemical weapons production facilities into chemical weapons destruction facilities shall ensure that the regime for the temporarily converted facilities is at least as stringent as the regime for chemical weapons production facilities that have not been converted.

19.   Chemical weapons production facilities converted into chemical weapons destruction facilities before entry into force of this Convention shall be declared under the category of chemical weapons production facilities.

They shall be subject to an initial visit by inspectors, who shall confirm the correctness of the information about these facilities. Verification that the conversion of these facilities was performed in such a manner as to render them inoperable as chemical weapons production facilities shall also be required, and shall fall within the framework of measures provided for the facilities that are to be rendered inoperable not later than 90 days after entry into force of this Convention.

20. A State Party that intends to carry out a conversion of chemical weapons production facilities shall submit to the Technical Secretariat, not later than 30 days after this Convention enters into force for it, or not later than 30 days after a decision has been taken for temporary conversion, a general facility conversion plan, and subsequently shall submit annual plans.

21. Should a State Party have the need to convert to a chemical weapons destruction facility an additional chemical weapons production facility that had been closed after this Convention entered into force for it, it shall inform the Technical Secretariat thereof not less than 150 days before conversion. The Technical Secretariat, in conjunction with the State Party, shall make sure that the necessary measures are taken to render that facility, after its conversion, inoperable as a chemical weapons production facility.

22. A facility converted for the destruction of chemical weapons shall not be more fit for resuming chemical weapons production than a chemical weapons production facility which has been closed and is under maintenance. Its reactivation shall require no less time than that required for a chemical weapons production facility that has been closed and is under maintenance.

23. Converted chemical weapons production facilities shall be destroyed not later than 10 years after entry into force of this Convention.

24. Any measures for the conversion of any given chemical weapons production facility shall be facility-specific and shall depend upon its individual characteristics.

25. The set of measures carried out for the purpose of converting a chemical weapons production facility into a chemical weapons destruction facility shall not be less than that which is provided for the disabling of other chemical weapons production facilities to be carried out not later than 90 days after this Convention enters into force for the State Party.

*Principles and methods related to destruction of a
chemical weapons production facility*

26. A State Party shall destroy equipment and buildings covered by the definition of a chemical weapons production facility as follows:

(*a*)   All specialized equipment and standard equipment shall be physically destroyed;

(*b*)   All specialized buildings and standard buildings shall be physically destroyed.

27. A State Party shall destroy facilities for producing unfilled chemical munitions and equipment for chemical weapons employment as follows:

(*a*)   Facilities used exclusively for production of non-chemical parts for chemical munitions or equipment specifically designed for use directly in connection with chemical weapons employment, shall be declared and destroyed. The destruction process and its verification shall be conducted according to the provisions of Article V and this Part of this Annex that govern destruction of chemical weapons production facilities;

(*b*)   All equipment designed or used exclusively for producing non-chemical parts for chemical munitions shall be physically destroyed. Such equipment, which includes specially designed moulds and metal-forming dies, may be brought to a special location for destruction;

(*c*)   All buildings and standard equipment used for such production activities shall be destroyed or converted for purposes not prohibited under this Convention, with confirmation, as necessary, through consultations and inspections as provided for under Article IX;

(*d*)   Activities for purposes not prohibited under this Convention may continue while destruction or conversion proceeds.

Order of destruction

28. The order of destruction of chemical weapons production facilities is based on the obligations specified in Article I and the other Articles of this Convention, including obligations regarding systematic on-site verification. It takes into account interests of States Parties for undiminished security during the destruction period; confidence-building in the early part of the destruction stage; gradual acquisition of experience in the course of destroying chemical weapons production facilities; and applicability irrespective of the actual characteristics of the facilities and the methods chosen for their destruction. The order of destruction is based on the principle of levelling out.

29. A State Party shall, for each destruction period, determine which chemical weapons production facilities are to be destroyed and carry out the destruction in such a way that not more than what is specified in paragraphs 30 and 31 remains at the end of each destruction period. A State Party is not precluded from destroying its facilities at a faster pace.

30. The following provisions shall apply to chemical weapons production facilities that produce Schedule 1 chemicals:

(a) A State Party shall start the destruction of such facilities not later than one year after this Convention enters into force for it, and shall complete it not later than 10 years after entry into force of this Convention. For a State which is a Party at the entry into force of this Convention, this overall period shall be divided into three separate destruction periods, namely, years 2-5, years 6-8, and years 9-10. For States which become a Party after entry into force of this Convention, the destruction periods shall be adapted, taking into account paragraphs 28 and 29;

(b) Production capacity shall be used as the comparison factor for such facilities. It shall be expressed in agent tonnes, taking into account the rules specified for binary chemical weapons;

(c) Appropriate agreed levels of production capacity shall be established for the end of the eighth year after entry into force of this Convention. Production capacity that exceeds the relevant level shall be destroyed in equal increments during the first two destruction periods;

(d) A requirement to destroy a given amount of capacity shall entail a requirement to destroy any other chemical weapons production facility that supplied the Schedule 1 facility or filled the Schedule 1 chemical produced there into munitions or devices;

(e) Chemical weapons production facilities that have been converted temporarily for destruction of chemical weapons shall continue to be subject to the obligation to destroy capacity according to the provisions of this paragraph.

31. A State Party shall start the destruction of chemical weapons production facilities not covered in paragraph 30 not later than one year after this Convention enters into force for it, and complete it not later than five years after entry into force of this Convention.

Detailed plans for destruction

32. Not less than 180 days before the destruction of a chemical weapons production facility starts, a State Party shall provide to the Technical Secretariat

the detailed plans for destruction of the facility, including proposed measures for verification of destruction referred to in paragraph 33 (*f*), with respect to, *inter alia*:

(*a*)   Timing of the presence of the inspectors at the facility to be destroyed; and

(*b*)   Procedures for verification of measures to be applied to each item on the declared inventory.

33.   The detailed plans for destruction of each chemical weapons production facility shall contain:

(*a*)   Detailed time schedule of the destruction process;

(*b*)   Layout of the facility;

(*c*)   Process flow diagram;

(*d*)   Detailed inventory of equipment, buildings and other items to be destroyed;

(*e*)   Measures to be applied to each item on the inventory;

(*f*)   Proposed measures for verification;

(*g*)   Security/safety measures to be observed during the destruction of the facility; and

(*h*)   Working and living conditions to be provided for inspectors.

34.   If a State Party intends to convert temporarily a chemical weapons production facility into a chemical weapons destruction facility, it shall notify the Technical Secretariat not less than 150 days before undertaking any conversion activities. The notification shall:

(*a*)   Specify the name, address, and location of the facility;

(*b*)   Provide a site diagram indicating all structures and areas that will be involved in the destruction of chemical weapons and also identify all structures of the chemical weapons production facility that are to be temporarily converted;

(*c*)   Specify the types of chemical weapons, and the type and quantity of chemical fill to be destroyed;

(*d*)   Specify the destruction method;

(*e*)   Provide a process flow diagram, indicating which portions of the production process and specialized equipment will be converted for the destruction of chemical weapons;

(*f*)   Specify the seals and inspection equipment potentially affected by the conversion, if applicable; and

(*g*)   Provide a schedule identifying: The time allocated to design, temporary conversion of the facility, installation of equipment, equipment check-out, destruction operations, and closure.

35.   In relation to the destruction of a facility that was temporarily converted for destruction of chemical weapons, information shall be provided in accordance with paragraphs 32 and 33.

Review of detailed plans

36.   On the basis of the detailed plan for destruction and proposed measures for verification submitted by the State Party, and on experience from previous inspections, the Technical Secretariat shall prepare a plan for verifying the destruction of the facility, consulting closely with the State Party. Any differences between the Technical Secretariat and the State Party concerning appropriate measures should be resolved through consultations. Any unresolved matters shall be forwarded to the Executive Council for appropriate action with a view to facilitating the full implementation of this Convention.

37.   To ensure that the provisions of Article V and this Part are fulfilled, the combined plans for destruction and verification shall be agreed upon between the Executive Council and the State Party. This agreement should be completed, not less than 60 days before the planned initiation of destruction.

38.   Each member of the Executive Council may consult with the Technical Secretariat on any issues regarding the adequacy of the combined plan for destruction and verification. If there are no objections by any member of the Executive Council, the plan shall be put into action.

39.   If there are any difficulties, the Executive Council shall enter into consultations with the State Party to reconcile them. If any difficulties remain unresolved they shall be referred to the Conference. The resolution of any differences over methods of destruction shall not delay the execution of other parts of the destruction plan that are acceptable.

40.   If agreement is not reached with the Executive Council on aspects of verification, or if the approved verification plan cannot be put into action, verification of destruction shall proceed through continuous monitoring with on-site instruments and physical presence of inspectors.

41.   Destruction and verification shall proceed according to the agreed plan. The verification shall not unduly interfere with the destruction process and shall be conducted through the presence of inspectors on-site to witness the destruction.

42. If required verification or destruction actions are not taken as planned, all States Parties shall be so informed.

C. VERIFICATION

Verification of declarations of chemical weapons production facilities through on-site inspection

43. The Technical Secretariat shall conduct an initial inspection of each chemical weapons production facility in the period between 90 and 120 days after this Convention enters into force for the State Party.

44. The purposes of the initial inspection shall be:

(*a*)   To confirm that the production of chemical weapons has ceased and that the facility has been inactivated in accordance with this Convention;

(*b*)   To permit the Technical Secretariat to familiarize itself with the measures that have been taken to cease production of chemical weapons at the facility;

(*c*)   To permit the inspectors to install temporary seals;

(*d*)   To permit the inspectors to confirm the inventory of buildings and specialized equipment;

(*e*)   To obtain information necessary for planning inspection activities at the facility, including use of tamper-indicating seals and other agreed equipment, which shall be installed pursuant to the detailed facility agreement for the facility; and

(*f*)   To conduct preliminary discussions regarding a detailed agreement on inspection procedures at the facility.

45. Inspectors shall employ, as appropriate, agreed seals, markers or other inventory control procedures to facilitate an accurate inventory of the declared items at each chemical weapons production facility.

46. Inspectors shall install such agreed devices as may be necessary to indicate if any resumption of production of chemical weapons occurs or if any declared item is removed. They shall take the necessary precaution not to hinder closure activities by the inspected State Party. Inspectors may return to maintain and verify the integrity of the devices.

47. If, on the basis of the initial inspection, the Director-General believes that additional measures are necessary to inactivate the facility in accordance with this Convention, the Director-General may request, not later than 135 days after this Convention enters into force for a State Party, that such measures be

implemented by the inspected State Party not later than 180 days after this Convention enters into force for it. At its discretion, the inspected State Party may satisfy the request. If it does not satisfy the request, the inspected State Party and the Director-General shall consult to resolve the matter.

Systematic verification of chemical weapons production facilities
and cessation of their activities

48. The purpose of the systematic verification of a chemical weapons production facility shall be to ensure that any resumption of production of chemical weapons or removal of declared items will be detected at this facility.

49. The detailed facility agreement for each chemical weapons production facility shall specify:

(*a*)   Detailed on-site inspection procedures, which may include:

  (i)   Visual examinations;

  (ii)   Checking and servicing of seals and other agreed devices; and

  (iii)   Obtaining and analysing samples;

(*b*)   Procedures for using tamper-indicating seals and other agreed equipment to prevent the undetected reactivation of the facility, which shall specify:

  (i)   The type, placement, and arrangements for installation; and

  (ii)   The maintenance of such seals and equipment; and

(*c*)   Other agreed measures.

50. The seals or other approved equipment provided for in a detailed agreement on inspection measures for that facility shall be placed not later than 240 days after this Convention enters into force for a State Party. Inspectors shall be permitted to visit each chemical weapons production facility for the installation of such seals or equipment.

51. During each calendar year, the Technical Secretariat shall be permitted to conduct up to four inspections of each chemical weapons production facility.

52. The Director-General shall notify the inspected State Party of his decision to inspect or visit a chemical weapons production facility 48 hours before the planned arrival of the inspection team at the facility for systematic inspections or visits.

In the case of inspections or visits to resolve urgent problems, this period may be shortened. The Director-General shall specify the purpose of the inspection or visit.

53. Inspectors shall, in accordance with the facility agreements, have unimpeded access to all parts of the chemical weapons production facilities. The items on the declared inventory to be inspected shall be chosen by the inspectors.

54. The guidelines for determining the frequency of systematic on-site inspections shall be considered and approved by the Conference pursuant to Article VIII, paragraph 21 (*i*). The particular production facility to be inspected shall be chosen by the Technical Secretariat in such a way as to preclude the prediction of precisely when the facility is to be inspected.

Verification of destruction of chemical weapons production facilities

55. The purpose of systematic verification of the destruction of chemical weapons production facilities shall be to confirm that the facility is destroyed in accordance with the obligations under this Convention and that each item on the declared inventory is destroyed in accordance with the agreed detailed plan for destruction.

56. When all items on the declared inventory have been destroyed, the Technical Secretariat shall confirm the declaration of the State Party to that effect. After this confirmation, the Technical Secretariat shall terminate the systematic verification of the chemical weapons production facility and shall promptly remove all devices and monitoring instruments installed by the inspectors.

57. After this confirmation, the State Party shall make the declaration that the facility has been destroyed.

Verification of temporary conversion of a chemical weapons production facility into a chemical weapons destruction facility

58. Not later than 90 days after receiving the initial notification of the intent to convert temporarily a production facility, the inspectors shall have the right to visit the facility to familiarize themselves with the proposed temporary conversion and to study possible inspection measures that will be required during the conversion.

59. Not later than 60 days after such a visit, the Technical Secretariat and the inspected State Party shall conclude a transition agreement containing additional inspection measures for the temporary conversion period. The transition agreement shall specify inspection procedures, including the use of seals, monitoring equipment, and inspections, that will provide confidence that no chemical weapons

production takes place during the conversion process. This agreement shall remain in force from the beginning of the temporary conversion activity until the facility begins operation as a chemical weapons destruction facility.

60. The inspected State Party shall not remove or convert any portion of the facility, or remove or modify any seal or other agreed inspection equipment that may have been installed pursuant to this Convention until the transition agreement has been concluded.

61. Once the facility begins operation as a chemical weapons destruction facility, it shall be subject to the provisions of Part IV (A) of this Annex applicable to chemical weapons destruction facilities. Arrangements for the pre-operation period shall be governed by the transition agreement.

62. During destruction operations the inspectors shall have access to all portions of the temporarily converted chemical weapons production facilities, including those that are not directly involved with the destruction of chemical weapons.

63. Before the commencement of work at the facility to convert it temporarily for chemical weapons destruction purposes and after the facility has ceased to function as a facility for chemical weapons destruction, the facility shall be subject to the provisions of this Part applicable to chemical weapons production facilities.

D. CONVERSION OF CHEMICAL WEAPONS PRODUCTION FACILITIES TO PURPOSES NOT PROHIBITED UNDER THIS CONVENTION

Procedures for requesting conversion

64. A request to use a chemical weapons production facility for purposes not prohibited under this Convention may be made for any facility that a State Party is already using for such purposes before this Convention enters into force for it, or that it plans to use for such purposes.

65. For a chemical weapons production facility that is being used for purposes not prohibited under this Convention when this Convention enters into force for the State Party, the request shall be submitted to the Director-General not later than 30 days after this Convention enters into force for the State Party. The request shall contain, in addition to data submitted in accordance with paragraph 1 (*h*) (iii), the following information:

(*a*) A detailed justification for the request;

(*b*) A general facility conversion plan that specifies:

(i)   The nature of the activity to be conducted at the facility;

(ii)   If the planned activity involves production, processing, or consumption of chemicals: the name of each of the chemicals, the flow diagram of the facility, and the quantities planned to be produced, processed, or consumed annually;

(iii)   Which buildings or structures are proposed to be used and what modifications are proposed, if any;

(iv)   Which buildings or structures have been destroyed or are proposed to be destroyed and the plans for destruction;

(v)   What equipment is to be used in the facility;

(vi)   What equipment has been removed and destroyed and what equipment is proposed to be removed and destroyed and the plans for its destruction;

(vii)   The proposed schedule for conversion, if applicable; and

(viii) The nature of the activity of each other facility operating at the site; and

(c)   A detailed explanation of how measures set forth in subparagraph (b), as well as any other measures proposed by the State Party, will ensure the prevention of standby chemical weapons production capability at the facility.

66.   For a chemical weapons production facility that is not being used for purposes not prohibited under this Convention when this Convention enters into force for the State Party, the request shall be submitted to the Director-General not later than 30 days after the decision to convert, but in no case later than four years after this Convention enters into force for the State Party. The request shall contain the following information:

(a)   A detailed justification for the request, including its economic needs;

(b)   A general facility conversion plan that specifies:

(i)   The nature of the activity planned to be conducted at the facility;

(ii)   If the planned activity involves production, processing, or consumption of chemicals: the name of each of the chemicals, the flow diagram of the facility, and the quantities planned to be produced, processed, or consumed annually;

(iii)   Which buildings or structures are proposed to be retained and what modifications are proposed, if any;

(iv)   Which buildings or structures have been destroyed or are proposed to be destroyed and the plans for destruction;

(v)   What equipment is proposed for use in the facility;

(vi)   What equipment is proposed to be removed and destroyed and the plans for its destruction;

(vii)   The proposed schedule for conversion; and

(viii)   The nature of the activity of each other facility operating at the site; and

(c)   A detailed explanation of how the measures set forth in subparagraph (b), as well as any other measures proposed by the State Party, will ensure the prevention of standby chemical weapons production capability at the facility.

67. The State Party may propose in its request any other measures it deems appropriate to build confidence.

Actions pending a decision

68. Pending a decision of the Conference, a State Party may continue to use for purposes not prohibited under this Convention a facility that was being used for such purposes before this Convention enters into force for it, but only if the State Party certifies in its request that no specialized equipment and no specialized buildings are being used and that the specialized equipment and specialized buildings have been rendered inactive using the methods specified in paragraph 13.

69. If the facility, for which the request was made, was not being used for purposes not prohibited under this Convention before this Convention enters into force for the State Party, or if the certification required in paragraph 68 is not made, the State Party shall cease immediately all activity pursuant to Article V, paragraph 4. The State Party shall close the facility in accordance with paragraph 13 not later than 90 days after this Convention enters into force for it.

Conditions for conversion

70. As a condition for conversion of a chemical weapons production facility for purposes not prohibited under this Convention, all specialized equipment at the facility must be destroyed and all special features of buildings and structures that distinguish them from buildings and structures normally used for purposes not prohibited under this Convention and not involving Schedule 1 chemicals must be eliminated.

71. A converted facility shall not be used:

(*a*)   For any activity involving production, processing, or consumption of a Schedule 1 chemical or a Schedule 2 chemical; or

(*b*)   For the production of any highly toxic chemical, including any highly toxic organophosphorus chemical, or for any other activity that would require special equipment for handling highly toxic or highly corrosive chemicals, unless the Executive Council decides that such production or activity would pose no risk to the object and purpose of this Convention, taking into account criteria for toxicity, corrosiveness and, if applicable, other technical factors, to be considered and approved by the Conference pursuant to Article VIII, paragraph 21 (*i*).

72. Conversion of a chemical weapons production facility shall be completed not later than six years after entry into force of this Convention.

Decisions by the Executive Council and the Conference

73. Not later than 90 days after receipt of the request by the Director-General, an initial inspection of the facility shall be conducted by the Technical Secretariat. The purpose of this inspection shall be to determine the accuracy of the information provided in the request, to obtain information on the technical characteristics of the proposed converted facility, and to assess the conditions under which use for purposes not prohibited under this Convention may be permitted. The Director-General shall promptly submit a report to the Executive Council, the Conference, and all States Parties containing his recommendations on the measures necessary to convert the facility to purposes not prohibited under this Convention and to provide assurance that the converted facility will be used only for purposes not prohibited under this Convention.

74. If the facility has been used for purposes not prohibited under this Convention before this Convention enters into force for the State Party, and is continuing to be in operation, but the measures required to be certified under paragraph 68 have not been taken, the Director-General shall immediately inform the Executive Council, which may require implementation of measures it deems

appropriate, *inter alia,* shut-down of the facility and removal of specialized equipment and modification of buildings or structures. The Executive Council shall stipulate the deadline for implementation of these measures and shall suspend consideration of the request pending their satisfactory completion. The facility shall be inspected promptly after the expiration of the deadline to determine whether the measures have been implemented. If not, the State Party shall be required to shut down completely all facility operations.

75. As soon as possible after receiving the report of the Director-General, the Conference, upon recommendation of the Executive Council, shall decide, taking into account the report and any views expressed by States Parties, whether to approve the request, and shall establish the conditions upon which approval is contingent. If any State Party objects to approval of the request and the associated conditions, consultations shall be undertaken among interested States Parties for up to 90 days to seek a mutually acceptable solution. A decision on the request and associated conditions, along with any proposed modifications thereto, shall be taken, as a matter of substance, as soon as possible after the end of the consultation period.

76. If the request is approved, a facility agreement shall be completed not later than 90 days after such a decision is taken. The facility agreement shall contain the conditions under which the conversion and use of the facility is permitted, including measures for verification. Conversion shall not begin before the facility agreement is concluded.

Detailed plans for conversion

77. Not less than 180 days before conversion of a chemical weapons production facility is planned to begin, the State Party shall provide the Technical Secretariat with the detailed plans for conversion of the facility, including proposed measures for verification of conversion, with respect to, *inter alia*:

(*a*)   Timing of the presence of the inspectors at the facility to be converted; and

(*b*)   Procedures for verification of measures to be applied to each item on the declared inventory.

78. The detailed plan for conversion of each chemical weapons production facility shall contain:

(*a*)   Detailed time schedule of the conversion process;

(*b*)   Layout of the facility before and after conversion;

(*c*)   Process flow diagram of the facility before, and as appropriate, after the conversion;

(*d*)   Detailed inventory of equipment, buildings and structures and other items to be destroyed and of the buildings and structures to be modified;

(*e*)   Measures to be applied to each item on the inventory, if any;

(*f*)   Proposed measures for verification;

(*g*)   Security/safety measures to be observed during the conversion of the facility; and

(*h*)   Working and living conditions to be provided for inspectors.

Review of detailed plans

79.   On the basis of the detailed plan for conversion and proposed measures for verification submitted by the State Party, and on experience from previous inspections, the Technical Secretariat shall prepare a plan for verifying the conversion of the facility, consulting closely with the State Party. Any differences between the Technical Secretariat and the State Party concerning appropriate measures shall be resolved through consultations. Any unresolved matters shall be forwarded to the Executive Council for appropriate action with a view to facilitate the full implementation of this Convention.

80.   To ensure that the provisions of Article V and this Part are fulfilled, the combined plans for conversion and verification shall be agreed upon between the Executive Council and the State Party. This agreement shall be completed not less than 60 days before conversion is planned to begin.

81.   Each member of the Executive Council may consult with the Technical Secretariat on any issue regarding the adequacy of the combined plan for conversion and verification. If there are no objections by any member of the Executive Council, the plan shall be put into action.

82.   If there are any difficulties, the Executive Council should enter into consultations with the State Party to reconcile them. If any difficulties remain unresolved, they should be referred to the Conference. The resolution of any differences over methods of conversion should not delay the execution of other parts of the conversion plan that are acceptable.

83.   If agreement is not reached with the Executive Council on aspects of verification, or if the approved verification plan cannot be put into action, verification of conversion shall proceed through continuous monitoring with on-site instruments and physical presence of inspectors.

84. Conversion and verification shall proceed according to the agreed plan. The verification shall not unduly interfere with the conversion process and shall be conducted through the presence of inspectors to confirm the conversion.

85. For the 10 years after the Director-General certifies that conversion is complete, the State Party shall provide to inspectors unimpeded access to the facility at any time. The inspectors shall have the right to observe all areas, all activities, and all items of equipment at the facility. The inspectors shall have the right to verify that the activities at the facility are consistent with any conditions established under this Section, by the Executive Council and the Conference. The inspectors shall also have the right, in accordance with provisions of Part II, Section E, of this Annex to receive samples from any area of the facility and to analyse them to verify the absence of Schedule 1 chemicals, their stable by-products and decomposition products and of Schedule 2 chemicals and to verify that the activities at the facility are consistent with any other conditions on chemical activities established under this Section, by the Executive Council and the Conference. The inspectors shall also have the right to managed access, in accordance with Part X, Section C, of this Annex, to the plant site at which the facility is located. During the 10-year period, the State Party shall report annually on the activities at the converted facility. Upon completion of the 10-year period, the Executive Council, taking into account recommendations of the Technical Secretariat, shall decide on the nature of continued verification measures.

86. Costs of verification of the converted facility shall be allocated in accordance with Article V, paragraph 19.

PART VI

ACTIVITIES NOT PROHIBITED UNDER THIS CONVENTION
IN ACCORDANCE WITH ARTICLE VI

REGIME FOR SCHEDULE 1 CHEMICALS AND FACILITIES
RELATED TO SUCH CHEMICALS

A.   GENERAL PROVISIONS

1.   A State Party shall not produce, acquire, retain or use Schedule 1 chemicals outside the territories of States Parties and shall not transfer such chemicals outside its territory except to another State Party.

2.   A State Party shall not produce, acquire, retain, transfer or use Schedule 1 chemicals unless:

(*a*)   The chemicals are applied to research, medical, pharmaceutical or protective purposes; and

(*b*)   The types and quantities of chemicals are strictly limited to those which can be justified for such purposes; and

(*c*)   The aggregate amount of such chemicals at any given time for such purposes is equal to or less than 1 tonne; and

(*d*)   The aggregate amount for such purposes acquired by a State Party in any year through production, withdrawal from chemical weapons stocks and transfer is equal to or less than 1 tonne.

B.   TRANSFERS

3.   A State Party may transfer Schedule 1 chemicals outside its territory only to another State Party and only for research, medical, pharmaceutical or protective purposes in accordance with paragraph 2.

4.   Chemicals transferred shall not be retransferred to a third State.

5.   Not less than 30 days before any transfer to another State Party both States Parties shall notify the Technical Secretariat of the transfer.

6.   Each State Party shall make a detailed annual declaration regarding transfers during the previous year. The declaration shall be submitted not later than 90 days after the end of that year and shall for each Schedule 1 chemical that has been transferred include the following information:

(*a*)   The chemical name, structural formula and Chemical Abstracts Service registry number, if assigned;

(*b*)   The quantity acquired from other States or transferred to other States Parties. For each transfer the quantity, recipient and purpose shall be included.

C. PRODUCTION

General principles for production

7.   Each State Party, during production under paragraphs 8 to 12, shall assign the highest priority to ensuring the safety of people and to protecting the environment. Each State Party shall conduct such production in accordance with its national standards for safety and emissions.

Single small-scale facility

8.   Each State Party that produces Schedule 1 chemicals for research, medical, pharmaceutical or protective purposes shall carry out the production at a single small-scale facility approved by the State Party, except as set forth in paragraphs 10, 11 and 12.

9.   The production at a single small-scale facility shall be carried out in reaction vessels in production lines not configured for continuous operation. The volume of such a reaction vessel shall not exceed 100 litres, and the total volume of all reaction vessels with a volume exceeding 5 litres shall not be more than 500 litres.

Other facilities

10.   Production of Schedule 1 chemicals in aggregate quantities not exceeding 10 kg per year may be carried out for protective purposes at one facility outside a single small-scale facility. This facility shall be approved by the State Party.

11.   Production of Schedule 1 chemicals in quantities of more than 100 g per year may be carried out for research, medical or pharmaceutical purposes outside a single small-scale facility in aggregate quantities not exceeding 10 kg per year per facility. These facilities shall be approved by the State Party.

12.   Synthesis of Schedule 1 chemicals for research, medical or pharmaceutical purposes, but not for protective purposes, may be carried out at laboratories in aggregate quantities less than 100 g per year per facility. These facilities shall not be subject to any obligation relating to declaration and verification as specified in Sections D and E.

D. DECLARATIONS

Single small-scale facility

13. Each State Party that plans to operate a single small-scale facility shall provide the Technical Secretariat with the precise location and a detailed technical description of the facility, including an inventory of equipment and detailed diagrams. For existing facilities, this initial declaration shall be provided not later than 30 days after this Convention enters into force for the State Party. Initial declarations on new facilities shall be provided not less than 180 days before operations are to begin.

14. Each State Party shall give advance notification to the Technical Secretariat of planned changes related to the initial declaration. The notification shall be submitted not less than 180 days before the changes are to take place.

15. A State Party producing Schedule 1 chemicals at a single small-scale facility shall make a detailed annual declaration regarding the activities of the facility for the previous year. The declaration shall be submitted not later than 90 days after the end of that year and shall include:

(*a*)   Identification of the facility;

(*b*)   For each Schedule 1 chemical produced, acquired, consumed or stored at the facility, the following information:

   (i)   The chemical name, structural formula and Chemical Abstracts Service registry number, if assigned;

   (ii)   The methods employed and quantity produced;

   (iii)   The name and quantity of precursors listed in Schedules 1, 2, or 3 used for production of Schedule 1 chemicals;

   (iv)   The quantity consumed at the facility and the purpose(s) of the consumption;

   (v)   The quantity received from or shipped to other facilities in the State Party. For each shipment the quantity, recipient and purpose should be included;

   (vi)   The maximum quantity stored at any time during the year; and

   (vii)   The quantity stored at the end of the year; and

(*c*)   Information on any changes at the facility during the year compared to previously submitted detailed technical descriptions of the facility including inventories of equipment and detailed diagrams.

16.   Each State Party producing Schedule 1 chemicals at a single small-scale facility shall make a detailed annual declaration regarding the projected activities and the anticipated production at the facility for the coming year. The declaration shall be submitted not less than 90 days before the beginning of that year and shall include:

(*a*)   Identification of the facility;

(*b*)   For each Schedule 1 chemical anticipated to be produced, consumed or stored at the facility, the following information:

(i)   The chemical name, structural formula and Chemical Abstracts Service registry number, if assigned;

(ii)   The quantity anticipated to be produced and the purpose of the production; and

(*c*)   Information on any anticipated changes at the facility during the year compared to previously submitted detailed technical descriptions of the facility including inventories of equipment and detailed diagrams.

Other facilities referred to in paragraphs 10 and 11

17.   For each facility, a State Party shall provide the Technical Secretariat with the name, location and a detailed technical description of the facility or its relevant part(s) as requested by the Technical Secretariat. The facility producing Schedule 1 chemicals for protective purposes shall be specifically identified. For existing facilities, this initial declaration shall be provided not later than 30 days after this Convention enters into force for the State Party. Initial declarations on new facilities shall be provided not less than 180 days before operations are to begin.

18.   Each State Party shall give advance notification to the Technical Secretariat of planned changes related to the initial declaration. The notification shall be submitted not less than 180 days before the changes are to take place.

19.   Each State Party shall, for each facility, make a detailed annual declaration regarding the activities of the facility for the previous year. The declaration shall be submitted not later than 90 days after the end of that year and shall include:

(*a*)   Identification of the facility;

(*b*) For each Schedule 1 chemical the following information:

  (i) The chemical name, structural formula and Chemical Abstracts Service registry number, if assigned;

  (ii) The quantity produced and, in case of production for protective purposes, methods employed;

  (iii) The name and quantity of precursors listed in Schedules 1, 2, or 3, used for production of Schedule 1 chemicals;

  (iv) The quantity consumed at the facility and the purpose of the consumption;

  (v) The quantity transferred to other facilities within the State Party. For each transfer the quantity, recipient and purpose should be included;

  (vi) The maximum quantity stored at any time during the year; and

  (vii) The quantity stored at the end of the year; and

(*c*) Information on any changes at the facility or its relevant parts during the year compared to previously submitted detailed technical description of the facility.

20. Each State Party shall, for each facility, make a detailed annual declaration regarding the projected activities and the anticipated production at the facility for the coming year. The declaration shall be submitted not less than 90 days before the beginning of that year and shall include:

(*a*) Identification of the facility;

(*b*) For each Schedule 1 chemical the following information:

  (i) The chemical name, structural formula and Chemical Abstracts Service registry number, if assigned; and

  (ii) The quantity anticipated to be produced, the time periods when the production is anticipated to take place and the purposes of the production; and

(*c*) Information on any anticipated changes at the facility or its relevant parts, during the year compared to previously submitted detailed technical descriptions of the facility.

E. VERIFICATION

Single small-scale facility

21. The aim of verification activities at the single small-scale facility shall be to verify that the quantities of Schedule 1 chemicals produced are correctly declared and, in particular, that their aggregate amount does not exceed 1 tonne.

22. The facility shall be subject to systematic verification through on-site inspection and monitoring with on-site instruments.

23. The number, intensity, duration, timing and mode of inspections for a particular facility shall be based on the risk to the object and purpose of this Convention posed by the relevant chemicals, the characteristics of the facility and the nature of the activities carried out there. Appropriate guidelines shall be considered and approved by the Conference pursuant to Article VIII, paragraph 21 (*i*).

24. The purpose of the initial inspection shall be to verify information provided concerning the facility, including verification of the limits on reaction vessels set forth in paragraph 9.

25. Not later than 180 days after this Convention enters into force for a State Party, it shall conclude a facility agreement, based on a model agreement, with the Organization, covering detailed inspection procedures for the facility.

26. Each State Party planning to establish a single small-scale facility after this Convention enters into force for it shall conclude a facility agreement, based on a model agreement, with the Organization, covering detailed inspection procedures for the facility before it begins operation or is used.

27. A model for agreements shall be considered and approved by the Conference pursuant to Article VIII, paragraph 21 (*i*).

Other facilities referred to in paragraphs 10 and 11

28. The aim of verification activities at any facility referred to in paragraphs 10 and 11 shall be to verify that:

(*a*) The facility is not used to produce any Schedule 1 chemical, except for the declared chemicals;

(*b*) The quantities of Schedule 1 chemicals produced, processed or consumed are correctly declared and consistent with needs for the declared purpose; and

(*c*) The Schedule 1 chemical is not diverted or used for other purposes.

29. The facility shall be subject to systematic verification through on-site inspection and monitoring with on-site instruments.

30. The number, intensity, duration, timing and mode of inspections for a particular facility shall be based on the risk to the object and purpose of this Convention posed by the quantities of chemicals produced, the characteristics of the facility and the nature of the activities carried out there. Appropriate guidelines shall be considered and approved by the Conference pursuant to Article VIII, paragraph 21 (*i*).

31. Not later than 180 days after this Convention enters into force for a State Party, it shall conclude facility agreements with the Organization, based on a model agreement covering detailed inspection procedures for each facility.

32. Each State Party planning to establish such a facility after entry into force of this Convention shall conclude a facility agreement with the Organization before the facility begins operation or is used.

PART VII

ACTIVITIES NOT PROHIBITED UNDER THIS CONVENTION
IN ACCORDANCE WITH ARTICLE VI

REGIME FOR SCHEDULE 2 CHEMICALS AND FACILITIES
RELATED TO SUCH CHEMICALS

A. DECLARATIONS

Declarations of aggregate national data

1.   The initial and annual declarations to be provided by each State Party pursuant to Article VI, paragraphs 7 and 8, shall include aggregate national data for the previous calendar year on the quantities produced, processed, consumed, imported and exported of each Schedule 2 chemical, as well as a quantitative specification of import and export for each country involved.

2.   Each State Party shall submit:

(*a*)   Initial declarations pursuant to paragraph 1 not later than 30 days after this Convention enters into force for it; and, starting in the following calendar year,

(*b*)   Annual declarations not later than 90 days after the end of the previous calendar year.

*Declarations of plant sites producing, processing or consuming
Schedule 2 chemicals*

3.   Initial and annual declarations are required for all plant sites that comprise one or more plant(s) which produced, processed or consumed during any of the previous three calendar years or is anticipated to produce, process or consume in the next calendar year more than:

(*a*)   1 kg of a chemical designated "*" in Schedule 2, part A;

(*b*)   100 kg of any other chemical listed in Schedule 2, part A; or

(*c*)   1 tonne of a chemical listed in Schedule 2, part B.

4.   Each State Party shall submit:

(*a*)   Initial declarations pursuant to paragraph 3 not later than 30 days after this Convention enters into force for it; and, starting in the following calendar year;

(*b*)   Annual declarations on past activities not later than 90 days after the end of the previous calendar year;

(*c*) Annual declarations on anticipated activities not later than 60 days before the beginning of the following calendar year. Any such activity additionally planned after the annual declaration has been submitted shall be declared not later than five days before this activity begins.

5. Declarations pursuant to paragraph 3 are generally not required for mixtures containing a low concentration of a Schedule 2 chemical. They are only required, in accordance with guidelines, in cases where the ease of recovery from the mixture of the Schedule 2 chemical and its total weight are deemed to pose a risk to the object and purpose of this Convention. These guidelines shall be considered and approved by the Conference pursuant to Article VIII, paragraph 21 (*i*).

6. Declarations of a plant site pursuant to paragraph 3 shall include:

(*a*) The name of the plant site and the name of the owner, company, or enterprise operating it;

(*b*) Its precise location including the address; and

(*c*) The number of plants within the plant site which are declared pursuant to Part VIII of this Annex.

7. Declarations of a plant site pursuant to paragraph 3 shall also include, for each plant which is located within the plant site and which falls under the specifications set forth in paragraph 3, the following information:

(*a*) The name of the plant and the name of the owner, company, or enterprise operating it;

(*b*) Its precise location within the plant site including the specific building or structure number, if any;

(*c*) Its main activities;

(*d*) Whether the plant:

    (i) Produces, processes, or consumes the declared Schedule 2 chemical(s);

    (ii) Is dedicated to such activities or multi-purpose; and

    (iii) Performs other activities with regard to the declared Schedule 2 chemical(s), including a specification of that other activity (e.g. storage); and

(*e*) The production capacity of the plant for each declared Schedule 2 chemical.

8. Declarations of a plant site pursuant to paragraph 3 shall also include the following information on each Schedule 2 chemical above the declaration threshold:

(*a*) The chemical name, common or trade name used by the facility, structural formula, and Chemical Abstracts Service registry number, if assigned;

(*b*) In the case of the initial declaration: the total amount produced, processed, consumed, imported and exported by the plant site in each of the three previous calendar years;

(*c*) In the case of the annual declaration on past activities: the total amount produced, processed, consumed, imported and exported by the plant site in the previous calendar year;

(*d*) In the case of the annual declaration on anticipated activities: the total amount anticipated to be produced, processed or consumed by the plant site in the following calendar year, including the anticipated time periods for production, processing or consumption; and

(*e*) The purposes for which the chemical was or will be produced, processed or consumed:

(i) Processing and consumption on site with a specification of the product types;

(ii) Sale or transfer within the territory or to any other place under the jurisdiction or control of the State Party, with a specification whether to other industry, trader or other destination and, if possible, of final product types;

(iii) Direct export, with a specification of the States involved; or

(iv) Other, including a specification of these other purposes.

Declarations on past production of Schedule 2 chemicals for chemical weapons purposes

9. Each State Party shall, not later than 30 days after this Convention enters into force for it, declare all plant sites comprising plants that produced at any time since 1 January 1946 a Schedule 2 chemical for chemical weapons purposes.

10. Declarations of a plant site pursuant to paragraph 9 shall include:

(*a*) The name of the plant site and the name of the owner, company, or enterprise operating it;

(*b*)   Its precise location including the address;

(*c*)   For each plant which is located within the plant site, and which falls under the specifications set forth in paragraph 9, the same information as required under paragraph 7, subparagraphs (*a*) to (*e*); and

(*d*)   For each Schedule 2 chemical produced for chemical weapons purposes:

   (i)   The chemical name, common or trade name used by the plant site for chemical weapons production purposes, structural formula, and Chemical Abstracts Service registry number, if assigned;

   (ii)   The dates when the chemical was produced and the quantity produced; and

   (iii)   The location to which the chemical was delivered and the final product produced there, if known.

Information to States Parties

11.   A list of plant sites declared under this Section together with the information provided under paragraphs 6, 7 (*a*), 7 (*c*), 7 (*d*) (i), 7 (*d*) (iii), 8 (*a*) and 10 shall be transmitted by the Technical Secretariat to States Parties upon request.

B.   VERIFICATION

General

12.   Verification provided for in Article VI, paragraph 4, shall be carried out through on-site inspection at those of the declared plant sites that comprise one or more plants which produced, processed or consumed during any of the previous three calendar years or are anticipated to produce, process or consume in the next calendar year more than:

(*a*)   10 kg of a chemical designated "*" in Schedule 2, part A;

(*b*)   1 tonne of any other chemical listed in Schedule 2, part A; or

(*c*)   10 tonnes of a chemical listed in Schedule 2, part B.

13.   The programme and budget of the Organization to be adopted by the Conference pursuant to Article VIII, paragraph 21 (*a*) shall contain, as a separate item, a programme and budget for verification under this Section. In the allocation of resources made available for verification under Article VI, the Technical Secretariat shall, during the first three years after the entry into force of this

Convention, give priority to the initial inspections of plant sites declared under Section A. The allocation shall thereafter be reviewed on the basis of the experience gained.

14. The Technical Secretariat shall conduct initial inspections and subsequent inspections in accordance with paragraphs 15 to 22.

Inspection aims

15. The general aim of inspections shall be to verify that activities are in accordance with obligations under this Convention and consistent with the information to be provided in declarations. Particular aims of inspections at plant sites declared under Section A shall include verification of:

(a) The absence of any Schedule 1 chemical, especially its production, except if in accordance with Part VI of this Annex;

(b) Consistency with declarations of levels of production, processing or consumption of Schedule 2 chemicals; and

(c) Non-diversion of Schedule 2 chemicals for activities prohibited under this Convention.

Initial inspections

16. Each plant site to be inspected pursuant to paragraph 12 shall receive an initial inspection as soon as possible but preferably not later than three years after entry into force of this Convention. Plant sites declared after this period shall receive an initial inspection not later than one year after production, processing or consumption is first declared. Selection of plant sites for initial inspections shall be made by the Technical Secretariat in such a way as to preclude the prediction of precisely when the plant site is to be inspected.

17. During the initial inspection, a draft facility agreement for the plant site shall be prepared unless the inspected State Party and the Technical Secretariat agree that it is not needed.

18. With regard to frequency and intensity of subsequent inspections, inspectors shall during the initial inspection assess the risk to the object and purpose of this Convention posed by the relevant chemicals, the characteristics of the plant site and the nature of the activities carried out there, taking into account, *inter alia,* the following criteria:

(a) The toxicity of the scheduled chemicals and of the end-products produced with it, if any;

(b) The quantity of the scheduled chemicals typically stored at the inspected site;

(*c*)   The quantity of feedstock chemicals for the scheduled chemicals typically stored at the inspected site;

(*d*)   The production capacity of the Schedule 2 plants; and

(*e*)   The capability and convertibility for initiating production, storage and filling of toxic chemicals at the inspected site.

Inspections

19.   Having received the initial inspection, each plant site to be inspected pursuant to paragraph 12 shall be subject to subsequent inspections.

20.   In selecting particular plant sites for inspection and in deciding on the frequency and intensity of inspections, the Technical Secretariat shall give due consideration to the risk to the object and purpose of this Convention posed by the relevant chemical, the characteristics of the plant site and the nature of the activities carried out there, taking into account the respective facility agreement as well as the results of the initial inspections and subsequent inspections.

21.   The Technical Secretariat shall choose a particular plant site to be inspected in such a way as to preclude the prediction of exactly when it will be inspected.

22.   No plant site shall receive more than two inspections per calendar year under the provisions of this Section. This, however, shall not limit inspections pursuant to Article IX.

Inspection procedures

23.   In addition to agreed guidelines, other relevant provisions of this Annex and the Confidentiality Annex, paragraphs 24 to 30 below shall apply.

24.   A facility agreement for the declared plant site shall be concluded not later than 90 days after completion of the initial inspection between the inspected State Party and the Organization unless the inspected State Party and the Technical Secretariat agree that it is not needed. It shall be based on a model agreement and govern the conduct of inspections at the declared plant site. The agreement shall specify the frequency and intensity of inspections as well as detailed inspection procedures, consistent with paragraphs 25 to 29.

25.   The focus of the inspection shall be the declared Schedule 2 plant(s) within the declared plant site. If the inspection team requests access to other parts of the plant site, access to these areas shall be granted in accordance with the obligation to provide clarification pursuant to Part II, paragraph 51, of this Annex and in

accordance with the facility agreement, or, in the absence of a facility agreement, in accordance with the rules of managed access as specified in Part X, Section C, of this Annex.

26. Access to records shall be provided, as appropriate, to provide assurance that there has been no diversion of the declared chemical and that production has been consistent with declarations.

27. Sampling and analysis shall be undertaken to check for the absence of undeclared scheduled chemicals.

28. Areas to be inspected may include:

(*a*) Areas where feed chemicals (reactants) are delivered or stored;

(*b*) Areas where manipulative processes are performed upon the reactants prior to addition to the reaction vessels;

(*c*) Feed lines as appropriate from the areas referred to in subparagraph (*a*) or subparagraph (*b*) to the reaction vessels together with any associated valves, flow meters, etc.;

(*d*) The external aspect of the reaction vessels and ancillary equipment;

(*e*) Lines from the reaction vessels leading to long- or short-term storage or to equipment further processing the declared Schedule 2 chemicals;

(*f*) Control equipment associated with any of the items under subparagraphs (*a*) to (*e*);

(*g*) Equipment and areas for waste and effluent handling;

(*h*) Equipment and areas for disposition of chemicals not up to specification.

29. The period of inspection shall not last more than 96 hours; however, extensions may be agreed between the inspection team and the inspected State Party.

Notification of inspection

30. A State Party shall be notified by the Technical Secretariat of the inspection not less than 48 hours before the arrival of the inspection team at the plant site to be inspected.

C. TRANSFERS TO STATES NOT PARTY TO THIS CONVENTION

31. Schedule 2 chemicals shall only be transferred to or received from States Parties. This obligation shall take effect three years after entry into force of this Convention.

32. During this interim three-year period, each State Party shall require an end-use certificate, as specified below, for transfers of Schedule 2 chemicals to States not Party to this Convention. For such transfers, each State Party shall adopt the necessary measures to ensure that the transferred chemicals shall only be used for purposes not prohibited under this Convention. *Inter alia*, the State Party shall require from the recipient State a certificate stating, in relation to the transferred chemicals:

(*a*) That they will only be used for purposes not prohibited under this Convention;

(*b*) That they will not be re-transferred;

(*c*) Their types and quantities;

(*d*) Their end-use(s); and

(*e*) The name(s) and address(es) of the end-user(s).

Part VIII

Activities not prohibited under this Convention in accordance with Article VI

Regime for Schedule 3 chemicals and facilities related to such chemicals

A. Declarations

Declarations of aggregate national data

1. The initial and annual declarations to be provided by a State Party pursuant to Article VI, paragraphs 7 and 8, shall include aggregate national data for the previous calendar year on the quantities produced, imported and exported of each Schedule 3 chemical, as well as a quantitative specification of import and export for each country involved.

2. Each State Party shall submit:

(a) Initial declarations pursuant to paragraph 1 not later than 30 days after this Convention enters into force for it; and, starting in the following calendar year,

(b) Annual declarations not later than 90 days after the end of the previous calendar year.

Declarations of plant sites producing Schedule 3 chemicals

3. Initial and annual declarations are required for all plant sites that comprise one or more plants which produced during the previous calendar year or are anticipated to produce in the next calendar year more than 30 tonnes of a Schedule 3 chemical.

4. Each State Party shall submit:

(a) Initial declarations pursuant to paragraph 3 not later than 30 days after this Convention enters into force for it; and, starting in the following calendar year;

(b) Annual declarations on past activities not later than 90 days after the end of the previous calendar year;

(c) Annual declarations on anticipated activities not later than 60 days before the beginning of the following calendar year. Any such activity additionally planned after the annual declaration has been submitted shall be declared not later than five days before this activity begins.

5. Declarations pursuant to paragraph 3 are generally not required for mixtures containing a low concentration of a Schedule 3 chemical. They are only required, in accordance with guidelines, in such cases where the ease of recovery from the mixture of the Schedule 3 chemical and its total weight are deemed to pose a risk to the object and purpose of this Convention. These guidelines shall be considered and approved by the Conference pursuant to Article VIII, paragraph 21 (*i*).

6. Declarations of a plant site pursuant to paragraph 3 shall include:

(*a*)   The name of the plant site and the name of the owner, company, or enterprise operating it;

(*b*)   Its precise location including the address; and

(*c*)   The number of plants within the plant site which are declared pursuant to Part VII of this Annex.

7. Declarations of a plant site pursuant to paragraph 3 shall also include, for each plant which is located within the plant site and which falls under the specifications set forth in paragraph 3, the following information:

(*a*)   The name of the plant and the name of the owner, company, or enterprise operating it;

(*b*)   Its precise location within the plant site, including the specific building or structure number, if any;

(*c*)   Its main activities.

8. Declarations of a plant site pursuant to paragraph 3 shall also include the following information on each Schedule 3 chemical above the declaration threshold:

(*a*)   The chemical name, common or trade name used by the facility, structural formula, and Chemical Abstracts Service registry number, if assigned;

(*b*)   The approximate amount of production of the chemical in the previous calendar year, or, in case of declarations on anticipated activities, anticipated for the next calendar year, expressed in the ranges: 30 to 200 tonnes, 200 to 1,000 tonnes, 1,000 to 10,000 tonnes, 10,000 to 100,000 tonnes, and above 100,000 tonnes; and

(*c*)   The purposes for which the chemical was or will be produced.

Declarations on past production of Schedule 3 chemicals for chemical weapons purposes

9.   Each State Party shall, not later than 30 days after this Convention enters into force for it, declare all plant sites comprising plants that produced at any time since 1 January 1946 a Schedule 3 chemical for chemical weapons purposes.

10.   Declarations of a plant site pursuant to paragraph 9 shall include:

(*a*)   The name of the plant site and the name of the owner, company, or enterprise operating it;

(*b*)   Its precise location including the address;

(*c*)   For each plant which is located within the plant site, and which falls under the specifications set forth in paragraph 9, the same information as required under paragraph 7, subparagraphs (*a*) to (*c*); and

(*d*)   For each Schedule 3 chemical produced for chemical weapons purposes:

   (i)   The chemical name, common or trade name used by the plant site for chemical weapons production purposes, structural formula, and Chemical Abstracts Service registry number, if assigned;

   (ii)   The dates when the chemical was produced and the quantity produced; and

   (iii)   The location to which the chemical was delivered and the final product produced there, if known.

Information to States Parties

11.   A list of plant sites declared under this Section together with the information provided under paragraphs 6, 7 (*a*), 7 (*c*), 8 (*a*) and 10 shall be transmitted by the Technical Secretariat to States Parties upon request.

B.   VERIFICATION

General

12.   Verification provided for in paragraph 5 of Article VI shall be carried out through on-site inspections at those declared plant sites which produced during the previous calendar year or are anticipated to produce in the next calendar year in excess of 200 tonnes aggregate of any Schedule 3 chemical above the declaration threshold of 30 tonnes.

13. The programme and budget of the Organization to be adopted by the Conference pursuant to Article VIII, paragraph 21 (*a*), shall contain, as a separate item, a programme and budget for verification under this Section taking into account Part VII, paragraph 13, of this Annex.

14. Under this Section, the Technical Secretariat shall randomly select plant sites for inspection through appropriate mechanisms, such as the use of specially designed computer software, on the basis of the following weighting factors:

(*a*)   Equitable geographical distribution of inspections; and

(*b*)   The information on the declared plant sites available to the Technical Secretariat, related to the relevant chemical, the characteristics of the plant site and the nature of the activities carried out there.

15. No plant site shall receive more than two inspections per year under the provisions of this Section. This, however, shall not limit inspections pursuant to Article IX.

16. In selecting plant sites for inspection under this Section, the Technical Secretariat shall observe the following limitation for the combined number of inspections to be received by a State Party per calendar year under this Part and Part IX of this Annex: the combined number of inspections shall not exceed three plus 5 per cent of the total number of plant sites declared by a State Party under both this Part and Part IX of this Annex, or 20 inspections, whichever of these two figures is lower.

Inspection aims

17. At plant sites declared under Section A, the general aim of inspections shall be to verify that activities are consistent with the information to be provided in declarations. The particular aim of inspections shall be the verification of the absence of any Schedule 1 chemical, especially its production, except if in accordance with Part VI of this Annex.

Inspection procedures

18. In addition to agreed guidelines, other relevant provisions of this Annex and the Confidentiality Annex, paragraphs 19 to 25 below shall apply.

19. There shall be no facility agreement, unless requested by the inspected State Party.

20. The focus of the inspections shall be the declared Schedule 3 plant(s) within the declared plant site. If the inspection team, in accordance with Part II, paragraph 51, of this Annex, requests access to other parts of the plant site for

clarification of ambiguities, the extent of such access shall be agreed between the inspection team and the inspected State Party.

21.   The inspection team may have access to records in situations in which the inspection team and the inspected State Party agree that such access will assist in achieving the objectives of the inspection.

22.   Sampling and on-site analysis may be undertaken to check for the absence of undeclared scheduled chemicals. In case of unresolved ambiguities, samples may be analysed in a designated off-site laboratory, subject to the inspected State Party's agreement.

23.   Areas to be inspected may include:

(a)   Areas where feed chemicals (reactants) are delivered or stored;

(b)   Areas where manipulative processes are performed upon the reactants prior to addition to the reaction vessel;

(c)   Feed lines as appropriate from the areas referred to in subparagraph (a) or subparagraph (b) to the reaction vessel together with any associated valves, flow meters, etc.;

(d)   The external aspect of the reaction vessels and ancillary equipment;

(e)   Lines from the reaction vessels leading to long- or short-term storage or to equipment further processing the declared Schedule 3 chemicals;

(f)   Control equipment associated with any of the items under subparagraphs (a) to (e);

(g)   Equipment and areas for waste and effluent handling;

(h)   Equipment and areas for disposition of chemicals not up to specification.

24.   The period of inspection shall not last more than 24 hours; however, extensions may be agreed between the inspection team and the inspected State Party.

Notification of inspection

25.   A State Party shall be notified by the Technical Secretariat of the inspection not less than 120 hours before the arrival of the inspection team at the plant site to be inspected.

C. TRANSFERS TO STATES NOT PARTY TO THIS CONVENTION

26. When transferring Schedule 3 chemicals to States not Party to this Convention, each State Party shall adopt the necessary measures to ensure that the transferred chemicals shall only be used for purposes not prohibited under this Convention. *Inter alia,* the State Party shall require from the recipient State a certificate stating, in relation to the transferred chemicals:

(*a*) That they will only be used for purposes not prohibited under this Convention;

(*b*) That they will not be re-transferred;

(*c*) Their types and quantities;

(*d*) Their end-use(s); and

(*e*) The name(s) and address(es) of the end-user(s).

27. Five years after entry into force of this Convention, the Conference shall consider the need to establish other measures regarding transfers of Schedule 3 chemicals to States not Party to this Convention.

PART IX

ACTIVITIES NOT PROHIBITED UNDER THIS CONVENTION
IN ACCORDANCE WITH ARTICLE VI

REGIME FOR OTHER CHEMICAL PRODUCTION FACILITIES

A. DECLARATIONS

List of other chemical production facilities

1. The initial declaration to be provided by each State Party pursuant to Article VI, paragraph 7, shall include a list of all plant sites that:

(*a*) Produced by synthesis during the previous calendar year more than 200 tonnes of unscheduled discrete organic chemicals; or

(*b*) Comprise one or more plants which produced by synthesis during the previous calendar year more than 30 tonnes of an unscheduled discrete organic chemical containing the elements phosphorus, sulfur or fluorine (hereinafter referred to as "PSF-plants" and "PSF-chemical").

2. The list of other chemical production facilities to be submitted pursuant to paragraph 1 shall not include plant sites that exclusively produced explosives or hydrocarbons.

3. Each State Party shall submit its list of other chemical production facilities pursuant to paragraph 1 as part of its initial declaration not later than 30 days after this Convention enters into force for it. Each State Party shall, not later than 90 days after the beginning of each following calendar year, provide annually the information necessary to update the list.

4. The list of other chemical production facilities to be submitted pursuant to paragraph 1 shall include the following information on each plant site:

(*a*) The name of the plant site and the name of the owner, company, or enterprise operating it;

(*b*) The precise location of the plant site including its address;

(*c*) Its main activities; and

(*d*) The approximate number of plants producing the chemicals specified in paragraph 1 in the plant site.

5. With regard to plant sites listed pursuant to paragraph 1 (*a*), the list shall also include information on the approximate aggregate amount of production of

the unscheduled discrete organic chemicals in the previous calendar year expressed in the ranges: under 1,000 tonnes, 1,000 to 10,000 tonnes and above 10,000 tonnes.

6.   With regard to plant sites listed pursuant to paragraph 1 (*b*), the list shall also specify the number of PSF-plants within the plant site and include information on the approximate aggregate amount of production of PSF-chemicals produced by each PSF-plant in the previous calendar year expressed in the ranges: under 200 tonnes, 200 to 1,000 tonnes, 1,000 to 10,000 tonnes and above 10,000 tonnes.

Assistance by the Technical Secretariat

7.   If a State Party, for administrative reasons, deems it necessary to ask for assistance in compiling its list of chemical production facilities pursuant to paragraph 1, it may request the Technical Secretariat to provide such assistance. Questions as to the completeness of the list shall then be resolved through consultations between the State Party and the Technical Secretariat.

Information to States Parties

8.   The lists of other chemical production facilities submitted pursuant to paragraph 1, including the information provided under paragraph 4, shall be transmitted by the Technical Secretariat to States Parties upon request.

B.   VERIFICATION

General

9.   Subject to the provisions of Section C, verification as provided for in Article VI, paragraph 6, shall be carried out through on-site inspection at:

(*a*) Plant sites listed pursuant to paragraph 1 (*a*); and

(*b*) Plant sites listed pursuant to paragraph 1 (*b*) that comprise one or more PSF-plants which produced during the previous calendar year more than 200 tonnes of a PSF-chemical.

10.   The programme and budget of the Organization to be adopted by the Conference pursuant to Article VIII, paragraph 21 (*a*), shall contain, as a separate item, a programme and budget for verification under this Section after its implementation has started.

11.   Under this Section, the Technical Secretariat shall randomly select plant sites for inspection through appropriate mechanisms, such as the use of specially designed computer software, on the basis of the following weighting factors:

(*a*) Equitable geographical distribution of inspections;

(*b*) The information on the listed plant sites available to the Technical Secretariat, related to the characteristics of the plant site and the activities carried out there; and

(*c*) Proposals by States Parties on a basis to be agreed upon in accordance with paragraph 25.

12. No plant site shall receive more than two inspections per year under the provisions of this Section. This, however, shall not limit inspections pursuant to Article IX.

13. In selecting plant sites for inspection under this Section, the Technical Secretariat shall observe the following limitation for the combined number of inspections to be received by a State Party per calendar year under this Part and Part VIII of this Annex: the combined number of inspections shall not exceed three plus 5 per cent of the total number of plant sites declared by a State Party under both this Part and Part VIII of this Annex, or 20 inspections, whichever of these two figures is lower.

Inspection aims

14. At plant sites listed under Section A, the general aim of inspections shall be to verify that activities are consistent with the information to be provided in declarations. The particular aim of inspections shall be the verification of the absence of any Schedule 1 chemical, especially its production, except if in accordance with Part VI of this Annex.

Inspection procedures

15. In addition to agreed guidelines, other relevant provisions of this Annex and the Confidentiality Annex, paragraphs 16 to 20 below shall apply.

16. There shall be no facility agreement, unless requested by the inspected State Party.

17. The focus of inspection at a plant site selected for inspection shall be the plant(s) producing the chemicals specified in paragraph 1, in particular the PSF-plants listed pursuant to paragraph 1 (*b*). The inspected State Party shall have the right to manage access to these plants in accordance with the rules of managed access as specified in Part X, Section C, of this Annex. If the inspection team, in accordance with Part II, paragraph 51, of this Annex, requests access to other parts of the plant site for clarification of ambiguities, the extent of such access shall be agreed between the inspection team and the inspected State Party.

18. The inspection team may have access to records in situations in which the inspection team and the inspected State Party agree that such access will assist in achieving the objectives of the inspection.

19. Sampling and on-site analysis may be undertaken to check for the absence of undeclared scheduled chemicals. In cases of unresolved ambiguities, samples may be analysed in a designated off-site laboratory, subject to the inspected State Party's agreement.

20. The period of inspection shall not last more than 24 hours; however, extensions may be agreed between the inspection team and the inspected State Party.

Notification of inspection

21. A State Party shall be notified by the Technical Secretariat of the inspection not less than 120 hours before the arrival of the inspection team at the plant site to be inspected.

C. IMPLEMENTATION AND REVIEW OF SECTION B

Implementation

22. The implementation of Section B shall start at the beginning of the fourth year after entry into force of this Convention unless the Conference, at its regular session in the third year after entry into force of this Convention, decides otherwise.

23. The Director-General shall, for the regular session of the Conference in the third year after entry into force of this Convention, prepare a report which outlines the experience of the Technical Secretariat in implementing the provisions of Parts VII and VIII of this Annex as well as of Section A of this Part.

24. At its regular session in the third year after entry into force of this Convention, the Conference, on the basis of a report of the Director-General, may also decide on the distribution of resources available for verification under Section B between "PSF-plants" and other chemical production facilities. Otherwise, this distribution shall be left to the expertise of the Technical Secretariat and be added to the weighting factors in paragraph 11.

25. At its regular session in the third year after entry into force of this Convention, the Conference, upon advice of the Executive Council, shall decide on which basis (e.g. regional) proposals by States Parties for inspections should be presented to be taken into account as a weighting factor in the selection process specified in paragraph 11.

Review

26. At the first special session of the Conference convened pursuant to Article VIII, paragraph 22, the provisions of this Part of the Verification Annex shall be re-examined in the light of a comprehensive review of the overall verification regime for the chemical industry (Article VI, Parts VII to IX of this Annex) on the basis of the experience gained. The Conference shall then make recommendations so as to improve the effectiveness of the verification regime.

PART X

CHALLENGE INSPECTIONS PURSUANT TO ARTICLE IX

A. DESIGNATION AND SELECTION OF INSPECTORS
AND INSPECTION ASSISTANTS

1.   Challenge inspections pursuant to Article IX shall only be performed by inspectors and inspection assistants especially designated for this function. In order to designate inspectors and inspection assistants for challenge inspections pursuant to Article IX, the Director-General shall, by selecting inspectors and inspection assistants from among the inspectors and inspection assistants for routine inspection activities, establish a list of proposed inspectors and inspection assistants. It shall comprise a sufficiently large number of inspectors and inspection assistants having the necessary qualification, experience, skill and training, to allow for flexibility in the selection of the inspectors, taking into account their availability, and the need for rotation. Due regard shall be paid also to the importance of selecting inspectors and inspection assistants on as wide a geographical basis as possible. The designation of inspectors and inspection assistants shall follow the procedures provided for under Part II, Section A, of this Annex.

2.   The Director-General shall determine the size of the inspection team and select its members taking into account the circumstances of a particular request. The size of the inspection team shall be kept to a minimum necessary for the proper fulfilment of the inspection mandate. No national of the requesting State Party or the inspected State Party shall be a member of the inspection team.

B.   PRE-INSPECTION ACTIVITIES

3.   Before submitting the inspection request for a challenge inspection, the State Party may seek confirmation from the Director-General that the Technical Secretariat is in a position to take immediate action on the request. If the Director-General cannot provide such confirmation immediately, he shall do so at the earliest opportunity, in keeping with the order of requests for confirmation. He shall also keep the State Party informed of when it is likely that immediate action can be taken. Should the Director-General reach the conclusion that timely action on requests can no longer be taken, he may ask the Executive Council to take appropriate action to improve the situation in the future.

Notification

4.   The inspection request for a challenge inspection to be submitted to the Executive Council and the Director-General shall contain at least the following information:

(*a*) The State Party to be inspected and, if applicable, the Host State;

(*b*) The point of entry to be used;

(*c*) The size and type of the inspection site;

(*d*) The concern regarding possible non-compliance with this Convention including a specification of the relevant provisions of this Convention about which the concern has arisen, and of the nature and circumstances of the possible non-compliance as well as all appropriate information on the basis of which the concern has arisen; and

(*e*) The name of the observer of the requesting State Party.

The requesting State Party may submit any additional information it deems necessary.

5.   The Director-General shall within one hour acknowledge to the requesting State Party receipt of its request.

6.   The requesting State Party shall notify the Director-General of the location of the inspection site in due time for the Director-General to be able to provide this information to the inspected State Party not less than 12 hours before the planned arrival of the inspection team at the point of entry.

7.   The inspection site shall be designated by the requesting State Party as specifically as possible by providing a site diagram related to a reference point with geographic coordinates, specified to the nearest second if possible. If possible, the requesting State Party shall also provide a map with a general indication of the inspection site and a diagram specifying as precisely as possible the requested perimeter of the site to be inspected.

8.   The requested perimeter shall:

(*a*) Run at least a 10 metre distance outside any buildings or other structures;

(*b*) Not cut through existing security enclosures; and

(*c*) Run at least a 10 metre distance outside any existing security enclosures that the requesting State Party intends to include within the requested perimeter.

9.   If the requested perimeter does not conform with the specifications of paragraph 8, it shall be redrawn by the inspection team so as to conform with that provision.

10. The Director-General shall, not less than 12 hours before the planned arrival of the inspection team at the point of entry, inform the Executive Council about the location of the inspection site as specified in paragraph 7.

11. Contemporaneously with informing the Executive Council according to paragraph 10, the Director-General shall transmit the inspection request to the inspected State Party including the location of the inspection site as specified in paragraph 7. This notification shall also include the information specified in Part II, paragraph 32, of this Annex.

12. Upon arrival of the inspection team at the point of entry, the inspected State Party shall be informed by the inspection team of the inspection mandate.

Entry into the territory of the inspected State Party or the Host State

13. The Director-General shall, in accordance with Article IX, paragraphs 13 to 18, dispatch an inspection team as soon as possible after an inspection request has been received. The inspection team shall arrive at the point of entry specified in the request in the minimum time possible, consistent with the provisions of paragraphs 10 and 11.

14. If the requested perimeter is acceptable to the inspected State Party, it shall be designated as the final perimeter as early as possible, but in no case later than 24 hours after the arrival of the inspection team at the point of entry. The inspected State Party shall transport the inspection team to the final perimeter of the inspection site. If the inspected State Party deems it necessary, such transportation may begin up to 12 hours before the expiry of the time period specified in this paragraph for the designation of the final perimeter. Transportation shall, in any case, be completed not later than 36 hours after the arrival of the inspection team at the point of entry.

15. For all declared facilities, the procedures in subparagraphs (*a*) and (*b*) shall apply. (For the purposes of this Part, "declared facility" means all facilities declared pursuant to Articles III, IV, and V. With regard to Article VI, "declared facility" means only facilities declared pursuant to Part VI of this Annex, as well as declared plants specified by declarations pursuant to Part VII, paragraphs 7 and 10 (*c*), and Part VIII, paragraphs 7 and 10 (*c*), of this Annex.)

(*a*) If the requested perimeter is contained within or conforms with the declared perimeter, the declared perimeter shall be considered the final perimeter. The final perimeter may, however, if agreed by the inspected State Party, be made smaller in order to conform with the perimeter requested by the requesting State Party.

(*b*) The inspected State Party shall transport the inspection team to the final perimeter as soon as practicable, but in any case shall ensure their arrival at the perimeter not later than 24 hours after the arrival of the inspection team at the point of entry.

Alternative determination of final perimeter

16. At the point of entry, if the inspected State Party cannot accept the requested perimeter, it shall propose an alternative perimeter as soon as possible, but in any case not later than 24 hours after the arrival of the inspection team at the point of entry. In case of differences of opinion, the inspected State Party and the inspection team shall engage in negotiations with the aim of reaching agreement on a final perimeter.

17. The alternative perimeter should be designated as specifically as possible in accordance with paragraph 8. It shall include the whole of the requested perimeter and should, as a rule, bear a close relationship to the latter, taking into account natural terrain features and man-made boundaries. It should normally run close to the surrounding security barrier if such a barrier exists. The inspected State Party should seek to establish such a relationship between the perimeters by a combination of at least two of the following means:

(*a*) An alternative perimeter that does not extend to an area significantly greater than that of the requested perimeter;

(*b*) An alternative perimeter that is a short, uniform distance from the requested perimeter;

(*c*) At least part of the requested perimeter is visible from the alternative perimeter.

18. If the alternative perimeter is acceptable to the inspection team, it shall become the final perimeter and the inspection team shall be transported from the point of entry to that perimeter. If the inspected State Party deems it necessary, such transportation may begin up to 12 hours before the expiry of the time period specified in paragraph 16 for proposing an alternative perimeter. Transportation shall, in any case, be completed not later than 36 hours after the arrival of the inspection team at the point of entry.

19. If a final perimeter is not agreed, the perimeter negotiations shall be concluded as early as possible, but in no case shall they continue more than 24 hours after the arrival of the inspection team at the point of entry. If no agreement is reached, the inspected State Party shall transport the inspection team to a location at the alternative perimeter. If the inspected State Party deems it necessary, such transportation may begin up to 12 hours before the expiry of the time period

specified in paragraph 16 for proposing an alternative perimeter. Transportation shall, in any case, be completed not later than 36 hours after the arrival of the inspection team at the point of entry.

20. Once at the location, the inspected State Party shall provide the inspection team with prompt access to the alternative perimeter to facilitate negotiations and agreement on the final perimeter and access within the final perimeter.

21. If no agreement is reached within 72 hours after the arrival of the inspection team at the location, the alternative perimeter shall be designated the final perimeter.

Verification of location

22. To help establish that the inspection site to which the inspection team has been transported corresponds to the inspection site specified by the requesting State Party, the inspection team shall have the right to use approved location-finding equipment and have such equipment installed according to its directions. The inspection team may verify its location by reference to local landmarks identified from maps. The inspected State Party shall assist the inspection team in this task.

Securing the site, exit monitoring

23. Not later than 12 hours after the arrival of the inspection team at the point of entry, the inspected State Party shall begin collecting factual information of all vehicular exit activity from all exit points for all land, air, and water vehicles of the requested perimeter. It shall provide this information to the inspection team upon its arrival at the alternative or final perimeter, whichever occurs first.

24. This obligation may be met by collecting factual information in the form of traffic logs, photographs, video recordings, or data from chemical evidence equipment provided by the inspection team to monitor such exit activity. Alternatively, the inspected State Party may also meet this obligation by allowing one or more members of the inspection team independently to maintain traffic logs, take photographs, make video recordings of exit traffic, or use chemical evidence equipment, and conduct other activities as may be agreed between the inspected State Party and the inspection team.

25. Upon the inspection team's arrival at the alternative perimeter or final perimeter, whichever occurs first, securing the site, which means exit monitoring procedures by the inspection team, shall begin.

26. Such procedures shall include: the identification of vehicular exits, the making of traffic logs, the taking of photographs, and the making of video recordings

by the inspection team of exits and exit traffic. The inspection team has the right to go, under escort, to any other part of the perimeter to check that there is no other exit activity.

27. Additional procedures for exit monitoring activities as agreed upon by the inspection team and the inspected State Party may include, *inter alia:*

(*a*) Use of sensors;

(*b*) Random selective access;

(*c*) Sample analysis.

28. All activities for securing the site and exit monitoring shall take place within a band around the outside of the perimeter, not exceeding 50 metres in width, measured outward.

29. The inspection team has the right to inspect on a managed access basis vehicular traffic exiting the site. The inspected State Party shall make every reasonable effort to demonstrate to the inspection team that any vehicle, subject to inspection, to which the inspection team is not granted full access, is not being used for purposes related to the possible non-compliance concerns raised in the inspection request.

30. Personnel and vehicles entering and personnel and personal passenger vehicles exiting the site are not subject to inspection.

31. The application of the above procedures may continue for the duration of the inspection, but may not unreasonably hamper or delay the normal operation of the facility.

Pre-inspection briefing and inspection plan

32. To facilitate development of an inspection plan, the inspected State Party shall provide a safety and logistical briefing to the inspection team prior to access.

33. The pre-inspection briefing shall be held in accordance with Part II, paragraph 37, of this Annex. In the course of the pre-inspection briefing, the inspected State Party may indicate to the inspection team the equipment, documentation, or areas it considers sensitive and not related to the purpose of the challenge inspection. In addition, personnel responsible for the site shall brief the inspection team on the physical layout and other relevant characteristics of the site. The inspection team shall be provided with a map or sketch drawn to scale showing all structures and significant geographic features at the site. The inspection team shall also be briefed on the availability of facility personnel and records.

34. After the pre-inspection briefing, the inspection team shall prepare, on the basis of the information available and appropriate to it, an initial inspection plan which specifies the activities to be carried out by the inspection team, including the specific areas of the site to which access is desired. The inspection plan shall also specify whether the inspection team will be divided into subgroups. The inspection plan shall be made available to the representatives of the inspected State Party and the inspection site. Its implementation shall be consistent with the provisions of Section C, including those related to access and activities.

Perimeter activities

35. Upon the inspection team's arrival at the final or alternative perimeter, whichever occurs first, the team shall have the right to commence immediately perimeter activities in accordance with the procedures set forth under this Section, and to continue these activities until the completion of the challenge inspection.

36. In conducting the perimeter activities, the inspection team shall have the right to:

(a) Use monitoring instruments in accordance with Part II, paragraphs 27 to 30, of this Annex;

(b) Take wipes, air, soil or effluent samples; and

(c) Conduct any additional activities which may be agreed between the inspection team and the inspected State Party.

37. The perimeter activities of the inspection team may be conducted within a band around the outside of the perimeter up to 50 metres in width measured outward from the perimeter. If the inspected State Party agrees, the inspection team may also have access to any building or structure within the perimeter band. All directional monitoring shall be oriented inward. For declared facilities, at the discretion of the inspected State Party, the band could run inside, outside, or on both sides of the declared perimeter.

C. CONDUCT OF INSPECTIONS

General rules

38. The inspected State Party shall provide access within the requested perimeter as well as, if different, the final perimeter. The extent and nature of access to a particular place or places within these perimeters shall be negotiated between the inspection team and the inspected State Party on a managed access basis.

39. The inspected State Party shall provide access within the requested perimeter as soon as possible, but in any case not later than 108 hours after the arrival of the inspection team at the point of entry in order to clarify the concern regarding possible non-compliance with this Convention raised in the inspection request.

40. Upon the request of the inspection team, the inspected State Party may provide aerial access to the inspection site.

41. In meeting the requirement to provide access as specified in paragraph 38, the inspected State Party shall be under the obligation to allow the greatest degree of access taking into account any constitutional obligations it may have with regard to proprietary rights or searches and seizures. The inspected State Party has the right under managed access to take such measures as are necessary to protect national security. The provisions in this paragraph may not be invoked by the inspected State Party to conceal evasion of its obligations not to engage in activities prohibited under this Convention.

42. If the inspected State Party provides less than full access to places, activities, or information, it shall be under the obligation to make every reasonable effort to provide alternative means to clarify the possible non-compliance concern that generated the challenge inspection.

43. Upon arrival at the final perimeter of facilities declared pursuant to Articles IV, V and VI, access shall be granted following the pre-inspection briefing and discussion of the inspection plan which shall be limited to the minimum necessary and in any event shall not exceed three hours. For facilities declared pursuant to Article III, paragraph 1 (*d*), negotiations shall be conducted and managed access commenced not later than 12 hours after arrival at the final perimeter.

44. In carrying out the challenge inspection in accordance with the inspection request, the inspection team shall use only those methods necessary to provide sufficient relevant facts to clarify the concern about possible non-compliance with the provisions of this Convention, and shall refrain from activities not relevant thereto. It shall collect and document such facts as are related to the possible non-compliance with this Convention by the inspected State Party, but shall neither seek nor document information which is clearly not related thereto, unless the inspected State Party expressly requests it to do so. Any material collected and subsequently found not to be relevant shall not be retained.

45. The inspection team shall be guided by the principle of conducting the challenge inspection in the least intrusive manner possible, consistent with the effective and timely accomplishment of its mission. Wherever possible, it shall begin with the least intrusive procedures it deems acceptable and proceed to more intrusive procedures only as it deems necessary.

Managed access

46. The inspection team shall take into consideration suggested modifications of the inspection plan and proposals which may be made by the inspected State Party, at whatever stage of the inspection including the pre-inspection briefing, to ensure that sensitive equipment, information or areas, not related to chemical weapons, are protected.

47. The inspected State Party shall designate the perimeter entry/exit points to be used for access. The inspection team and the inspected State Party shall negotiate: the extent of access to any particular place or places within the final and requested perimeters as provided in paragraph 48; the particular inspection activities, including sampling, to be conducted by the inspection team; the performance of particular activities by the inspected State Party; and the provision of particular information by the inspected State Party.

48. In conformity with the relevant provisions in the Confidentiality Annex the inspected State Party shall have the right to take measures to protect sensitive installations and prevent disclosure of confidential information and data not related to chemical weapons. Such measures may include, *inter alia*:

(*a*) Removal of sensitive papers from office spaces;

(*b*) Shrouding of sensitive displays, stores, and equipment;

(*c*) Shrouding of sensitive pieces of equipment, such as computer or electronic systems;

(*d*) Logging off of computer systems and turning off of data indicating devices;

(*e*) Restriction of sample analysis to presence or absence of chemicals listed in Schedules 1, 2 and 3 or appropriate degradation products;

(*f*) Using random selective access techniques whereby the inspectors are requested to select a given percentage or number of buildings of their choice to inspect; the same principle can apply to the interior and content of sensitive buildings;

(*g*) In exceptional cases, giving only individual inspectors access to certain parts of the inspection site.

49. The inspected State Party shall make every reasonable effort to demonstrate to the inspection team that any object, building, structure, container or vehicle to which the inspection team has not had full access, or which has been protected in accordance with paragraph 48, is not used for purposes related to the possible non-compliance concerns raised in the inspection request.

50. This may be accomplished by means of, *inter alia*, the partial removal of a shroud or environmental protection cover, at the discretion of the inspected State Party, by means of a visual inspection of the interior of an enclosed space from its entrance, or by other methods.

51. In the case of facilities declared pursuant to Articles IV, V and VI, the following shall apply:

(*a*) For facilities with facility agreements, access and activities within the final perimeter shall be unimpeded within the boundaries established by the agreements;

(*b*) For facilities without facility agreements, negotiation of access and activities shall be governed by the applicable general inspection guidelines established under this Convention;

(*c*) Access beyond that granted for inspections under Articles IV, V and VI shall be managed in accordance with procedures of this section.

52. In the case of facilities declared pursuant to Article III, paragraph 1 (*d*), the following shall apply: if the inspected State Party, using procedures of paragraphs 47 and 48, has not granted full access to areas or structures not related to chemical weapons, it shall make every reasonable effort to demonstrate to the inspection team that such areas or structures are not used for purposes related to the possible non-compliance concerns raised in the inspection request.

Observer

53. In accordance with the provisions of Article IX, paragraph 12, on the participation of an observer in the challenge inspection, the requesting State Party shall liaise with the Technical Secretariat to coordinate the arrival of the observer at the same point of entry as the inspection team within a reasonable period of the inspection team's arrival.

54. The observer shall have the right throughout the period of inspection to be in communication with the embassy of the requesting State Party located in the inspected State Party or in the Host State or, in the case of absence of an embassy, with the requesting State Party itself. The inspected State Party shall provide means of communication to the observer.

55. The observer shall have the right to arrive at the alternative or final perimeter of the inspection site, wherever the inspection team arrives first, and to have access to the inspection site as granted by the inspected State Party. The observer shall have the right to make recommendations to the inspection team, which the team shall take into account to the extent it deems appropriate. Throughout the inspection, the inspection team shall keep the observer informed about the conduct of the inspection and the findings.

56. Throughout the in-country period, the inspected State Party shall provide or arrange for the amenities necessary for the observer such as communication means, interpretation services, transportation, working space, lodging, meals and medical care. All the costs in connection with the stay of the observer on the territory of the inspected State Party or the Host State shall be borne by the requesting State Party.

Duration of inspection

57. The period of inspection shall not exceed 84 hours, unless extended by agreement with the inspected State Party.

D. POST-INSPECTION ACTIVITIES

Departure

58. Upon completion of the post-inspection procedures at the inspection site, the inspection team and the observer of the requesting State Party shall proceed promptly to a point of entry and shall then leave the territory of the inspected State Party in the minimum time possible.

Reports

59. The inspection report shall summarize in a general way the activities conducted by the inspection team and the factual findings of the inspection team, particularly with regard to the concerns regarding possible non-compliance with this Convention cited in the request for the challenge inspection, and shall be limited to information directly related to this Convention. It shall also include an assessment by the inspection team of the degree and nature of access and cooperation granted to the inspectors and the extent to which this enabled them to fulfil the inspection mandate. Detailed information relating to the concerns regarding possible non-compliance with this Convention cited in the request for the challenge inspection shall be submitted as an Appendix to the final report and be retained within the Technical Secretariat under appropriate safeguards to protect sensitive information.

60. The inspection team shall, not later than 72 hours after its return to its primary work location, submit a preliminary inspection report, having taken into account, *inter alia,* paragraph 17 of the Confidentiality Annex, to the Director-General. The Director-General shall promptly transmit the preliminary inspection report to the requesting State Party, the inspected State Party and to the Executive Council.

61. A draft final inspection report shall be made available to the inspected State Party not later than 20 days after the completion of the challenge inspection.

The inspected State Party has the right to identify any information and data not related to chemical weapons which should, in its view, due to its confidential character, not be circulated outside the Technical Secretariat. The Technical Secretariat shall consider proposals for changes to the draft final inspection report made by the inspected State Party and, using its own discretion, wherever possible, adopt them. The final report shall then be submitted not later than 30 days after the completion of the challenge inspection to the Director-General for further distribution and consideration in accordance with Article IX, paragraphs 21 to 25.

PART XI

INVESTIGATIONS IN CASES OF ALLEGED USE OF CHEMICAL WEAPONS

A. GENERAL

1. Investigations of alleged use of chemical weapons, or of alleged use of riot control agents as a method of warfare, initiated pursuant to Articles IX or X, shall be conducted in accordance with this Annex and detailed procedures to be established by the Director-General.

2. The following additional provisions address specific procedures required in cases of alleged use of chemical weapons.

B. PRE-INSPECTION ACTIVITIES

Request for an investigation

3. The request for an investigation of an alleged use of chemical weapons to be submitted to the Director-General, to the extent possible, should include the following information:

(*a*) The State Party on whose territory use of chemical weapons is alleged to have taken place;

(*b*) The point of entry or other suggested safe routes of access;

(*c*) Location and characteristics of the areas where chemical weapons are alleged to have been used;

(*d*) When chemical weapons are alleged to have been used;

(*e*) Types of chemical weapons believed to have been used;

(*f*) Extent of alleged use;

(*g*) Characteristics of the possible toxic chemicals;

(*h*) Effects on humans, animals and vegetation;

(*i*) Request for specific assistance, if applicable.

4. The State Party which has requested an investigation may submit at any time any additional information it deems necessary.

Notification

5. The Director-General shall immediately acknowledge receipt to the requesting State Party of its request and inform the Executive Council and all States Parties.

6. If applicable, the Director-General shall notify the State Party on whose territory an investigation has been requested. The Director-General shall also notify other States Parties if access to their territories might be required during the investigation.

Assignment of inspection team

7. The Director-General shall prepare a list of qualified experts whose particular field of expertise could be required in an investigation of alleged use of chemical weapons and constantly keep this list updated. This list shall be communicated, in writing, to each State Party not later than 30 days after entry into force of this Convention and after each change to the list. Any qualified expert included in this list shall be regarded as designated unless a State Party, not later than 30 days after its receipt of the list, declares its non-acceptance in writing.

8. The Director-General shall select the leader and members of an inspection team from the inspectors and inspection assistants already designated for challenge inspections taking into account the circumstances and specific nature of a particular request. In addition, members of the inspection team may be selected from the list of qualified experts when, in the view of the Director-General, expertise not available among inspectors already designated is required for the proper conduct of a particular investigation.

9. When briefing the inspection team, the Director-General shall include any additional information provided by the requesting State Party, or any other sources, to ensure that the inspection can be carried out in the most effective and expedient manner.

Dispatch of inspection team

10. Immediately upon the receipt of a request for an investigation of alleged use of chemical weapons the Director-General shall, through contacts with the relevant States Parties, request and confirm arrangements for the safe reception of the team.

11. The Director-General shall dispatch the team at the earliest opportunity, taking into account the safety of the team.

12. If the inspection team has not been dispatched within 24 hours from the receipt of the request, the Director-General shall inform the Executive Council and the States Parties concerned about the reasons for the delay.

Briefings

13. The inspection team shall have the right to be briefed by representatives of the inspected State Party upon arrival and at any time during the inspection.

14. Before the commencement of the inspection the inspection team shall prepare an inspection plan to serve, *inter alia,* as a basis for logistic and safety arrangements. The inspection plan shall be updated as need arises.

C.   CONDUCT OF INSPECTIONS

Access

15. The inspection team shall have the right of access to any and all areas which could be affected by the alleged use of chemical weapons. It shall also have the right of access to hospitals, refugee camps and other locations it deems relevant to the effective investigation of the alleged use of chemical weapons. For such access, the inspection team shall consult with the inspected State Party.

Sampling

16. The inspection team shall have the right to collect samples of types, and in quantities it considers necessary. If the inspection team deems it necessary, and if so requested by it, the inspected State Party shall assist in the collection of samples under the supervision of inspectors or inspection assistants. The inspected State Party shall also permit and cooperate in the collection of appropriate control samples from areas neighbouring the site of the alleged use and from other areas as requested by the inspection team.

17. Samples of importance in the investigation of alleged use include toxic chemicals, munitions and devices, remnants of munitions and devices, environmental samples (air, soil, vegetation, water, snow, etc.) and biomedical samples from human or animal sources (blood, urine, excreta, tissue etc.).

18. If duplicate samples cannot be taken and the analysis is performed at off-site laboratories, any remaining sample shall, if so requested, be returned to the inspected State Party after the completion of the analysis.

Extension of inspection site

19. If the inspection team during an inspection deems it necessary to extend the investigation into a neighbouring State Party, the Director-General shall notify that State Party about the need for access to its territory and request and confirm arrangements for the safe reception of the team.

Extension of inspection duration

20. If the inspection team deems that safe access to a specific area relevant to the investigation is not possible, the requesting State Party shall be informed immediately. If necessary, the period of inspection shall be extended until safe access can be provided and the inspection team will have concluded its mission.

Interviews

21. The inspection team shall have the right to interview and examine persons who may have been affected by the alleged use of chemical weapons. It shall also have the right to interview eyewitnesses of the alleged use of chemical weapons and medical personnel, and other persons who have treated or have come into contact with persons who may have been affected by the alleged use of chemical weapons. The inspection team shall have access to medical histories, if available, and be permitted to participate in autopsies, as appropriate, of persons who may have been affected by the alleged use of chemical weapons.

D. REPORTS

Procedures

22. The inspection team shall, not later than 24 hours after its arrival on the territory of the inspected State Party, send a situation report to the Director-General. It shall further throughout the investigation send progress reports as necessary.

23. The inspection team shall, not later than 72 hours after its return to its primary work location, submit a preliminary report to the Director-General. The final report shall be submitted to the Director-General not later than 30 days after its return to its primary work location. The Director-General shall promptly transmit the preliminary and final reports to the Executive Council and to all States Parties.

Contents

24. The situation report shall indicate any urgent need for assistance and any other relevant information. The progress reports shall indicate any further need for assistance that might be identified during the course of the investigation.

25. The final report shall summarize the factual findings of the inspection, particularly with regard to the alleged use cited in the request. In addition, a report of an investigation of an alleged use shall include a description of the investigation process, tracing its various stages, with special reference to:

(*a*) The locations and time of sampling and on-site analyses; and

(*b*) Supporting evidence, such as the records of interviews, the results of medical examinations and scientific analyses, and the documents examined by the inspection team.

26. If the inspection team collects through, *inter alia,* identification of any impurities or other substances during laboratory analysis of samples taken, any information in the course of its investigation that might serve to identify the origin of any chemical weapons used, that information shall be included in the report.

E.   STATES NOT PARTY TO THIS CONVENTION

27. In the case of alleged use of chemical weapons involving a State not Party to this Convention or in territory not controlled by a State Party, the Organization shall closely cooperate with the Secretary-General of the United Nations. If so requested, the Organization shall put its resources at the disposal of the Secretary-General of the United Nations.

ANNEX ON THE PROTECTION OF CONFIDENTIAL INFORMATION
("CONFIDENTIALITY ANNEX")
CONTENTS

A. GENERAL PRINCIPLES FOR THE HANDLING OF CONFIDENTIAL INFORMATION

1. The obligation to protect confidential information shall pertain to the verification of both civil and military activities and facilities. Pursuant to the general obligations set forth in Article VIII, the Organization shall:

(*a*) Require only the minimum amount of information and data necessary for the timely and efficient carrying out of its responsibilities under this Convention;

(*b*) Take the necessary measures to ensure that inspectors and other staff members of the Technical Secretariat meet the highest standards of efficiency, competence, and integrity;

(*c*) Develop agreements and regulations to implement the provisions of this Convention and shall specify as precisely as possible the information to which the Organization shall be given access by a State Party.

2. The Director-General shall have the primary responsibility for ensuring the protection of confidential information. The Director-General shall establish a stringent regime governing the handling of confidential information by the Technical Secretariat, and in doing so, shall observe the following guidelines:

(*a*) Information shall be considered confidential if:

(i) It is so designated by the State Party from which the information was obtained and to which the information refers; or

(ii) In the judgement of the Director-General, its unauthorized disclosure could reasonably be expected to cause damage to the State Party to which it refers or to the mechanisms for implementation of this Convention;

(*b*) All data and documents obtained by the Technical Secretariat shall be evaluated by the appropriate unit of the Technical Secretariat in order to establish whether they contain confidential information. Data required by States Parties to be assured of the continued compliance with this Convention by other States Parties shall be routinely provided to them. Such data shall encompass:

(i) The initial and annual reports and declarations provided by States Parties under Articles III, IV, V and VI, in accordance with the provisions set forth in the Verification Annex;

(ii) General reports on the results and effectiveness of verification activities; and

(iii)   Information to be supplied to all States Parties in accordance with the provisions of this Convention;

(c)   No information obtained by the Organization in connection with the implementation of this Convention shall be published or otherwise released, except, as follows:

(i)   General information on the implementation of this Convention may be compiled and released publicly in accordance with the decisions of the Conference or the Executive Council;

(ii)   Any information may be released with the express consent of the State Party to which the information refers;

(iii)   Information classified as confidential shall be released by the Organization only through procedures which ensure that the release of information only occurs in strict conformity with the needs of this Convention. Such procedures shall be considered and approved by the Conference pursuant to Article VIII, paragraph 21 (i);

(d)   The level of sensitivity of confidential data or documents shall be established, based on criteria to be applied uniformly in order to ensure their appropriate handling and protection. For this purpose, a classification system shall be introduced, which by taking account of relevant work undertaken in the preparation of this Convention shall provide for clear criteria ensuring the inclusion of information into appropriate categories of confidentiality and the justified durability of the confidential nature of information. While providing for the necessary flexibility in its implementation the classification system shall protect the rights of States Parties providing confidential information. A classification system shall be considered and approved by the Conference pursuant to Article VIII, paragraph 21 (i);

(e)   Confidential information shall be stored securely at the premises of the Organization. Some data or documents may also be stored with the National Authority of a State Party. Sensitive information, including, *inter alia*, photographs, plans and other documents required only for the inspection of a specific facility may be kept under lock and key at this facility;

(f)   To the greatest extent consistent with the effective implementation of the verification provisions of this Convention, information shall be handled and stored by the Technical Secretariat in a form that precludes direct identification of the facility to which it pertains;

(g)   The amount of confidential information removed from a facility shall be kept to the minimum necessary for the timely and effective implementation of the verification provisions of this Convention; and (*h*)   Access to confidential information shall be regulated in accordance with its classification. The dissemination of confidential information within the Organization shall be strictly on a need-to-know basis.

3.   The Director-General shall report annually to the Conference on the implementation of the regime governing the handling of confidential information by the Technical Secretariat.

4.   Each State Party shall treat information which it receives from the Organization in accordance with the level of confidentiality established for that information. Upon request, a State Party shall provide details on the handling of information provided to it by the Organization.

B.   EMPLOYMENT AND CONDUCT OF PERSONNEL IN THE TECHNICAL SECRETARIAT

5.   Conditions of staff employment shall be such as to ensure that access to and handling of confidential information shall be in conformity with the procedures established by the Director-General in accordance with Section A.

6.   Each position in the Technical Secretariat shall be governed by a formal position description that specifies the scope of access to confidential information, if any, needed in that position.

7.   The Director-General, the inspectors and the other members of the staff shall not disclose even after termination of their functions to any unauthorized persons any confidential information coming to their knowledge in the performance of their official duties. They shall not communicate to any State, organization or person outside the Technical Secretariat any information to which they have access in connection with their activities in relation to any State Party.

8.   In the discharge of their functions inspectors shall only request the information and data which are necessary to fulfil their mandate. They shall not make any records of information collected incidentally and not related to verification of compliance with this Convention.

9.   The staff shall enter into individual secrecy agreements with the Technical Secretariat covering their period of employment and a period of five years after it is terminated.

10.   In order to avoid improper disclosures, inspectors and staff members shall be appropriately advised and reminded about security considerations and of the possible penalties that they would incur in the event of improper disclosure.

11.   Not less than 30 days before an employee is given clearance for access to confidential information that refers to activities on the territory or in any other

place under the jurisdiction or control of a State Party, the State Party concerned shall be notified of the proposed clearance. For inspectors the notification of a proposed designation shall fulfil this requirement.

12. In evaluating the performance of inspectors and any other employees of the Technical Secretariat, specific attention shall be given to the employee's record regarding protection of confidential information.

C. MEASURES TO PROTECT SENSITIVE INSTALLATIONS AND PREVENT DISCLOSURE OF CONFIDENTIAL DATA IN THE COURSE OF ON-SITE VERIFICATION ACTIVITIES

13. States Parties may take such measures as they deem necessary to protect confidentiality, provided that they fulfil their obligations to demonstrate compliance in accordance with the relevant Articles and the Verification Annex. When receiving an inspection, the State Party may indicate to the inspection team the equipment, documentation or areas that it considers sensitive and not related to the purpose of the inspection.

14. Inspection teams shall be guided by the principle of conducting on-site inspections in the least intrusive manner possible consistent with the effective and timely accomplishment of their mission. They shall take into consideration proposals which may be made by the State Party receiving the inspection, at whatever stage of the inspection, to ensure that sensitive equipment or information, not related to chemical weapons, is protected.

15. Inspection teams shall strictly abide by the provisions set forth in the relevant Articles and Annexes governing the conduct of inspections. They shall fully respect the procedures designed to protect sensitive installations and to prevent the disclosure of confidential data.

16. In the elaboration of arrangements and facility agreements, due regard shall be paid to the requirement of protecting confidential information. Agreements on inspection procedures for individual facilities shall also include specific and detailed arrangements with regard to the determination of those areas of the facility to which inspectors are granted access, the storage of confidential information on-site, the scope of the inspection effort in agreed areas, the taking of samples and their analysis, the access to records and the use of instruments and continuous monitoring equipment.

17. The report to be prepared after each inspection shall only contain facts relevant to compliance with this Convention. The report shall be handled in accordance with the regulations established by the Organization governing the handling of confidential information. If necessary, the information contained in the report shall be processed into less sensitive forms before it is transmitted outside the Technical Secretariat and the inspected State Party.

D. Procedures in Case of Breaches or Alleged Breaches of Confidentiality

18. The Director-General shall establish necessary procedures to be followed in case of breaches or alleged breaches of confidentiality, taking into account recommendations to be considered and approved by the Conference pursuant to Article VIII, paragraph 21 (*i*).

19. The Director-General shall oversee the implementation of individual secrecy agreements. The Director-General shall promptly initiate an investigation if, in his judgement, there is sufficient indication that obligations concerning the protection of confidential information have been violated. The Director-General shall also promptly initiate an investigation if an allegation concerning a breach of confidentiality is made by a State Party.

20. The Director-General shall impose appropriate punitive and disciplinary measures on staff members who have violated their obligations to protect confidential information. In cases of serious breaches, the immunity from jurisdiction may be waived by the Director-General.

21. States Parties shall, to the extent possible, cooperate and support the Director-General in investigating any breach or alleged breach of confidentiality and in taking appropriate action in case a breach has been established.

22. The Organization shall not be held liable for any breach of confidentiality committed by members of the Technical Secretariat.

23. For breaches involving both a State Party and the Organization, a "Commission for the settlement of disputes related to confidentiality", set up as a subsidiary organ of the Conference, shall consider the case. This Commission shall be appointed by the Conference. Rules governing its composition and operating procedures shall be adopted by the Conference at its first session.

Selective Index

SELECTIVE INDEX

The following sample entries illustrate the way in which the various sections of the Convention are referred to in the *Selective Index*:

Preamble	Preamble
II.2	Article II, paragraph 2
AC.A.2	Annex on Chemicals, part A, paragraph 2
VA.X.27, 48	Verification Annex, part X, paragraphs 27 and 48
CA.2(*h*)	Confidentiality Annex, subparagraph 2(*h*).

An underlined entry signifies the primary source of information on a subject:

<u>IV</u>	The article dealing with chemical weapons

The following acronyms appear in the *Selective Index*:

CSP	Conference of the States Parties
ICJ	International Court of Justice
ISP	inspected State Party
IUPAC	International Union of Pure and Applied Chemistry
OPCW	Organization for the Prohibition of Chemical Weapons
PSF	phosphorus, sulfur or fluorine (per VA.IX)
UN	United Nations

The *Selective Index* does not contain any references to the "Text on the Establishment of a Preparatory Commission".

A

Abandoned chemical weapons

Declarations	III.1(*b*), VA.IV(B).8-10
Definition	II.6
Destruction	I.3, VA.IV(B).2, 13-18
Regime for	VA.IV(B).2, 8-18

(see also *Chemical weapons, buried*; *Old chemical weapons*)

F

Facilities

Definition VA.I.6

(see also *Binary chemical weapons; Chemical weapons destruction facilities; Chemical weapons production facilities; Conversion; Other chemical production facilities; Plants/plant sites; Schedule 1, 2 or 3 chemicals/facilities; Single small-scale facility*)

Facility agreements VA.I.7, VA.II.38, 45, VA.III.1-9

Challenge inspection VA.X.51

Chemical weapons destruction facilities . . . . VA.III.4-7, VA.IV(A).51, 59-60, 63, 70

Chemical weapons production facilities . . . . VA.V.44(*e*), 49-50, 53, 76

Confidentiality CA.16

Model VA.III.8, VA.VI.25-27, 31, VA.VII.24

Other chemical production facilities VA.IX.16

Schedule 1 . . . . VA.VI.25-26, 31-32

Schedule 2 . . . . VA.VII.17, 20, 24-25

Schedule 3 . . . . VA.VIII.19

Storage facilities . . . . VA.IV(A).42, 46, 49, 63

Transitional . . . . VA.III.6-7, VA.IV(A).51

(see also *Access*)

G

Geneva Protocol . . . . Preamble, XIII, XVI.3

Guidelines

Confidentiality . . . . CA.2(*a*)-(*h*) (see also *Confidential information/ confidentiality*)

Old chemical weapons, usability of . . . . VA.IV(B).5

Preparatory Commission develops . . . . VIII.21(*i*)

Schedules of chemicals . . . . AC.A, VA.VII.5 (see also *Schedule 1, 2 or 3 chemicals/facilities*)

(see also *CSP; Executive Council; Inspection; Technical Secretariat*)

H

Headquarters agreement VIII.50

Herbicides . . . . Preamble

Host State (inspections) VA.I.8-9, 12, VA.II.9-44, 61, VA.X.4, 13, 54, 56

188

I

N

O

S

V

Verification

Litho in United Nations, New York   ISBN 92-1-142213-2   United Nations publication
38988—October 1994—2,800   Sales No. E.95.IX.2